"There's great courage and hope and charity amongst all of us to overcome any evil. That's the fundamental story of Paul Rusesabagina—the greatness of the human spirit. The second thing is that in the wider political story of Rwanda, human beings are a more important commodity to the world than oil or gold or silver or platinum or diamonds. When we start realizing that it's worthwhile to go in and rescue people, to stop these sorts of humanitarian crises going on, then I think the world will be a much better place."
                                        —Terry George, 2004

HOTEL RWANDA

Bringing the True Story of an African Hero to Film

Edited by
Terry George

Screenplay Written by
Keir Pearson & Terry George

Newmarket Press New York

This book is published in the United States of America.

First Edition

10 9 8 7 6 5 4 3 2 1
ISBN 1-55704-670-0 (pb)

10 9 8 7 6 5 4 3 2 1
ISBN 1-55704-671-9 (hc)

Library of Congress Cataloging-in-Publication Data available upon request.

QUANTITY PURCHASES
Companies, professional groups, clubs, and other organizations may qualify for special
terms when ordering quantities of this title. For information, write Special Sales Department, Newmarket Press, 18 East 48th Street, New York, NY 10017; call (212) 832-3575;
fax (212) 832-3629; or e-mail info@newmarketpress.com.

www.newmarketpress.com

Manufactured in the United States of America.

Contents

For the dead of Murambi.

I will never forget.

—Terry George

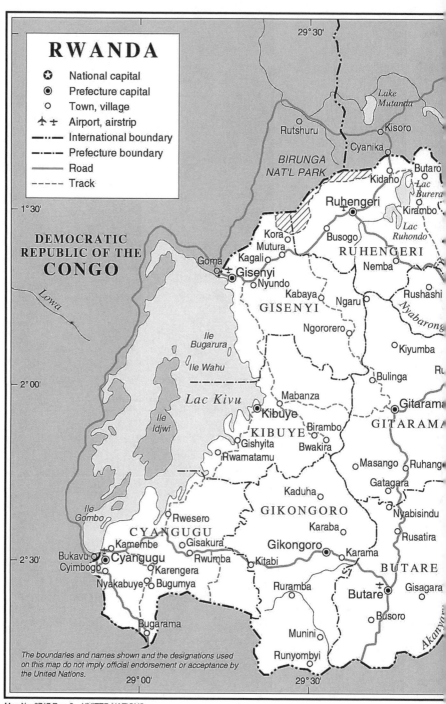

RWANDA

✪ National capital
◉ Prefecture capital
○ Town, village
✈ ✈ Airport, airstrip
–·–·– International boundary
–·–·– Prefecture boundary
——— Road
– – – – Track

29° 30'

Lake Mutanda

DEMOCRATIC
REPUBLIC OF THE
CONGO

Rutshuru   Kisoro

Cyanika

BIRUNGA
NAT'L PARK   Butaro

Kidaho   Lac
                Burera

Ruhengeri   Kirambo

Kora   Busogo   Lac
Mutura   Ruhondo

Goma Kagali   RUHENGERI

Gisenyi   Nemba

Nyundo

Kabaya   Ngaru   Rushashi

GISENYI

Ngororero

Kiyumba

Bulinga

Mabanza

Lac Kivu   Kibuye   Gitarama

Ile
Idjwi   Birambo   GITARAMA

KIBUYE

Gishyita   Bwakira

Rwamatamu

Masango Ruhang

Gatagara

Kaduha

Ile
Gombo   Rwesero   GIKONGORO

Nyabisindu

CYANGUGU   Karaba

Rusatira

Kamembe   Gisakura   Gikongoro Karama

Bukavu Cyangugu   Rwumba   Kitabi   BUTARE

Cyimbogo

Karengera   Gisagara

Nyakabuye Bugumya   Ruramba   Butare

Busoro

Bugarama

Munini

The boundaries and names shown and the designations used
on this map do not imply official endorsement or acceptance by
the United Nations.   29° 00'   29° 30'

Runyombyi

1° 30'

2° 00'

2° 30'

Lowa

Ile
Bugarura

Ile Wahu

Nyabarong

Akany

Map No. 3717 Rev. 9   UNITED NATIONS
January 2004

I.
A Story That
Needed To Be Told

Gianluigi Guercia

Paul Rusesabagina at the Hotel des Mille Collines in Kigali, Rwanda, in the room in which he, his family and forty other people lived during the genocide of 1994.

The Beginning

Keir Pearson

In early 1999, I had recently finished film school at NYU and was barely making ends meet as a documentary film editor in New York City. A novelist friend of mine, by the name of John Robinson, had recently returned from seven years in Africa and visited me in my Park Slope, Brooklyn, apartment. After catching up, he told me an amazing story that rocked me to my core. He told me about a Rwandan hotel manager, named Paul Rusesabagina, who wheeled and dealed to save a thousand people in a hotel during the height of the country's horrific genocide in 1994. John was living in neighboring Tanzania at the time of the genocide and had heard about Paul and his hotel, the Hotel Mille Collines, from a shocking news report broadcast over Radio France International by a Rwandan journalist trapped there. The journalist described how the hotel was completely surrounded by the murderous Interahamwe (the Hutu militia) and how the hotel's refugees were forced to drink water from the swimming pool to survive. John said I should look into this. I agreed. Little did I know at that time but the story of Paul's heroics at the Mille Collines would come to consume my life for the next five years.

As I did my initial research, I learned startling facts about the Rwandan genocide. The United Nations had 2,500 troops in Rwanda at the beginning of 1994 to monitor a peace agreement between Hutu extremists and Tutsi rebels. The UN high command was repeatedly warned that the Hutu government was preparing for genocide, yet no steps were taken to prevent it.

Courtesy of Keir Pearson

Keir Pearson meeting with Thomas Kamalindi, the Rwandan reporter who was trapped in the Mille Collines during the genocide. His broadcast over Radio France International was heard by John Robinson.

When the massacres finally began in April of that year, the UN General in Rwanda requested additional troops. He believed that with a total of 5,000 troops he could put a stop to the killing engulfing the country with devastating speed. Instead, the UN chiefs in New York decided to pull the majority of his troops and leave only a small token force as mere observers to the atrocities. In short, the great Western Democracies had decided to do nothing because they didn't want another embarrassment like Somalia. As a result, nearly 1,000,000 Rwandans were slaughtered in the spring of 1994.

I was struck by the fact that at a time when the superpowers of the world decided to do nothing, one man made a difference. For me, Paul Rusesabagina's story needed to be told. I wanted to use the medium I loved, film, to make people aware of something that they too easily ignored in 1994.

My first call was to the Rwandan embassy in Washington, D.C. A woman answered the phone, and I told her I was interested in Paul Rusesabagina and the events surrounding the Mille Collines. I asked her if she could put me in touch with someone who could help. She replied that she was a survivor from the hotel. She readily agreed to meet, so I got on the next train to D.C. and took her to a local restaurant for dinner. Over the next four hours, she never touched her food once as she told me the most harrowing story of how she, as a Tutsi, survived systematic rape and made it to the Mille Collines Hotel with her young son (she asked that I never use her name). I was amazed at how open she was about the most painful of details. Why tell me? I had no official credentials. I wasn't attached to any news organization or studio. I was just a guy with a backpack that expressed an interest. This was something that I would encounter time and again as I researched and wrote the script: The Rwandans I met wanted to be heard.

After more interviews in the United States, I tracked Paul down through Alison Des Forges at Human Rights Watch. Alison has written the most comprehensive book about the Rwandan genocide titled *Leave None to Tell the Story*. She gave me Paul's number in Belgium where he was living with his family and working as a taxi cab driver. I called him and once again was pleased at how readily he agreed to meet me.

My plan was to fly to Belgium and interview Paul and then continue on to Rwanda where I would interview more genocide survivors, especially those that were trapped in the Mille Collines. Then on my way home, I would stop in Belgium once again for another meeting with Paul. But the problem was that I was flat broke. My girlfriend at the time, who is now my wife, solved this by giving me her frequent-flier miles and loaning me the money. The other problem was that most Rwandans speak Kinyarwandan, French, and possibly a little Swahili. I speak none of them, so doing interviews would be next to impossible. I called my old friend John Robinson, who is fluent in both Swahili and French, and begged him to come along. John agreed to come and trans-

John Robinson standing in front of the Rwandan Genocide Museum under construction in Gisozi, October 2000.

late. He also agreed to pay for his travel expenses out of his own pocket. Every struggling writer should be fortunate enough to have people like this in their life.

In the fall of 2000, John and I flew to Belgium and met Paul Rusesabagina, the man I had wanted to meet for more than a year, in a grassy, tree-lined suburb of Brussels. He was the consummate host and invited us into his home, serving us coffee as we sat in his living room. He introduced us to his wife, Tatiana, and the nieces he adopted after their parents, Tatiana's brother and sister-in-law, were killed in the genocide. As the conversation turned to the genocide, Paul began recounting his life leading up to and during these horrific events. We talked for hours. By evening, Paul had to return to work, so we said our goodbyes and promised to stop in again on our return journey.

After this first meeting, what struck me most about Paul was

Courtesy of Keir Pearson

Cement tombs at the Rwandan Genocide Museum with Kigali, Rwanda, in the background, October 2000.

his diplomacy and seemingly unflappable poise. It was easy to see how someone like that could be persuasive and effective in any kind of dealings, even with genocidal killers.

Next, John and I flew to Kigali, Rwanda, and upon arriving, checked into the Hotel Mille Collines, the very hotel in which Paul saved the refugees. Our first stop was the genocide memorial in Gisozi, which was still under construction at the time. We got out of our taxi and were milling about a bunch of sealed cement tombs when one of the construction workers approached us. He told us that some 20,000 victims of the genocide were buried in the tombs. As we stared riveted by the cement memorials, he asked us why we were there. I explained that I was researching a script that I wanted to write about the Rwandan genocide. So he said that we should follow him.

He led us down a hill towards two tin shacks, and as we got closer, a smell hit me that I can only describe as death. He opened

Courtesy of Keir Pearson

The tin shack at the base of the Genocide Museum where the clothes of genocide victims were kept, October 2000.

the door to the first shack, and John and I stepped in. The day was hot, but in the shack, the heat was suffocating and the stench of death clung to us like sweat. John gagged and quickly left as I stood standing there staring at a mound of clothes, caked with dried blood, torn by apparent machete slashes that had ended their owners' lives. The worker explained that they were saving these to put in the museum once it was finished. The cement tombs outside, he said, didn't do justice to the carnage of the genocide. Then he walked me over to the next shack. John decided to remain outside. In there, hundreds of bones were neatly arranged in stacks. The skulls, many of the small ones obviously children's, had gaping holes where the fatal blow was delivered. I don't know what made me stand there and look at them while John headed back to the car, but I guess it was because I had come all this way to bear witness to the horror of the genocide, so

Courtesy of Keir Pearson

The church at Ntarama where some 5,000 Rwandans were slaughtered. The victims in the church were left where they died as a reminder of what happened, October 2000.

I might as well stare the beast in the face. Well, maybe not the beast itself but definitely its aftermath.

Over the coming weeks John and I would visit many genocide sites. The country is literally overrun with them, many of them churches. In particular was a church in Ntarama where the victims were left where they fell, their remains still clothed, a constant reminder for all those who pass. We saw bridges where victims were thrown to their deaths, and wells where helpless Tutsis were buried alive, crushed by the weight of bodies piling on top of them. John and I constantly reminded each other that genocide is not something specific to Africa. It has happened all over the world and continues to happen today.

Most of my time though was spent interviewing survivors from the genocide, especially those from the Mille Collines, with John translating. I had a list of names compiled from several sources. As in the past, I found Rwandans more than willing to talk, and soon people were approaching us, including employees at the hotel that were present during the genocide. Weeks were filled hearing hundreds of hours of testimonials from countless survivors from all walks of life. We talked to government ministers, mayors, lawyers, doctors, businessmen, policemen, shopkeepers, street vendors, drivers, farmers, aid workers, and especially journalists. Much to John's delight, we interviewed the very journalist who broadcast the shocking news report from the hotel that John heard back in 1994.

Then it was time to head home. It's safe to say that my time in Rwanda changed me profoundly, but I'm not sure I have the words to describe how. All I know is that the images, the people, and the smells of the place are burned into my mind forever.

On our return trip, John and I once again stopped in Brussels and met with Paul Rusesabagina to fact-check much of what we heard and have him answer a few more questions. Then I returned home to pore over the mountain of material and write.

The entire next year was devoted to getting a script out on *Hotel Rwanda*, the most daunting aspect being an overwhelming responsibility I felt toward the survivors I had met, especially Paul. I still had to work as a documentary editor, only writing at night and on the weekends. But every three months I saved enough money so I could take time off to write during the week.

By the fall of 2001, I finished writing *Hotel Rwanda*. It had been two years since John first told me about Paul Rusesabagina and the Hotel Mille Collines, and I had spent untold hours and more money than I could afford to get to this point. Needless to say, I was more than a little nervous as I boarded a plane and took the script to Los Angeles.

Luckily, I heard that veteran filmmaker and Oscar-nominated screenwriter Terry George was looking for a project on Africa. We met in New York (as it turns out our offices were only blocks away from each other in Manhattan), and I told him this was a project that he needed to do. It was a story that had to be told. He read the script and fell in love with the project. We both agreed that the purpose of the film was to reach a wide audience, an audience that probably knew nothing about the Rwandan genocide, and make them aware. By the summer of 2002, Terry took the first crucial step in getting the film made—he paid for Paul's life rights out of his own pocket. Soon the project would consume Terry the same way it had consumed me.

Don Cheadle, Joaquin Phoenix, Terry George, and Paul Rusesabagina on set during filming in South Africa.

My Promise

Terry George

For several years now, I've wanted to make a film that said something about life in modern Africa. The sheer scale of that continent's suffering—its poverty, wealth, beauty, and horror—moved and excited me like no other topic. I was continually warned that Hollywood has almost no interest in African topics. Such films don't get made, I was told, because they are a financial liability. In the fall of 2001, a television editor named Keir Pearson introduced me to the story of Paul Rusesabagina. It was a story I felt had to be told.

In 1994, Rusesabagina was working as a hotel manager in Kigali, Rwanda's capital. He lived a comfortable middle-class life, mingling easily with both the Rwandan elite and the diplomatic community. He had a beautiful young wife, Tatiana, and four healthy children. His marriage bridged the country's ethnic divide: He is Hutu, his wife is Tutsi.

On the night of April 6 of that year, the Hutu president of Rwanda was assassinated, his plane shot from the sky. Within minutes, the slaughter had begun. Hutu extremists used the president's death as an excuse for the systematic eradication of the Tutsi. Over the course of 100 days, more than 800,000 souls were murdered—most of them hacked to death with farm implements.

In the days that followed, Rusesabagina turned the four-star Mille Collines hotel in Kigali into a sanctuary for more than 1,200 Tutsi and moderate Hutu refugees. Over the next three months, he bartered beer, wine, money, and favors to keep the killers of the Hutu army and militia at bay. He lost not a single soul while the roads outside the hotel were littered with the dead.

In January 2002, I traveled to Brussels to meet Paul and his family. (He fled there after the genocide, and had set up a small taxi company.) He is a distinguished man, perfectly groomed, polite, and precise. I told him I wanted to make his story into a feature film. We signed a deal.

Back in New York, Pearson and I hammered out a script and circulated it in Los Angeles. The response was consistent: "Wonderful story, wonderful script, not for us." The studio word was that they'd do it if we got Denzel Washington or Will Smith for the lead. Both passed. Paul called regularly to check up on progress. I grew more embarrassed with each empty update.

Then, in January 2003, Paul called to say he and Tatiana planned to return to Rwanda for the first time since they had left. I went along. As he stepped off the plane in Kigali, Paul was mobbed by friends and family. At the Mille Collines Hotel, the staff rushed to hug the man who had saved their lives. Everywhere we went, Paul and Tatiana were greeted as heroes. But the joy of their return was often overshadowed by the memories. When they met friends and relatives, every conversation seemed to end the same way: ". . . but they are all dead now" or ". . . then they were all killed."

One afternoon, Paul took me to visit a memorial at a place called Murambi. The Murambi technical college sits atop a hill in southern Rwanda. It is a modern glass and concrete structure, impressive by central African standards. The lush green hills all around are dotted with small huts and carefully tended banana groves. Behind the main building is a series of long brick buildings. Once they held classrooms. Over the course of four days that April, some 40,000 people were slaughtered here. Today, hundreds of corpses are laid out on platforms inside the rooms as a shocking memorial to the Rwandan genocide. Immediately after the massacres, the bodies were covered in lime. The chemical preserved the corpses and turned them white—the color that

Frank Connor

Alex Kitman Ho walks Paul Rusesabagina to the set to see it for the first time.

would have guaranteed their safety during the genocide. The bodies are frozen in the contortions of their death throes. Children's hands are upheld in hopeless defense. Men's skulls lie cracked open by machetes. As I left that sacred place, a guide led me to the guest book. I signed my name and stared at the comments column, paralyzed, desperate for something relevant to say. Tears welled up in my eyes as I scribbled, then read what I had written: "I promise to tell the story of the genocide to the world."

But there was no good news upon my return to New York. We weren't making progress with the studios; however, my agent had sent the script to the producer Alex Ho *(Platoon, Ali)*. We met, and he told me he believed in the script and loved my idea of Don Cheadle as the lead. He set to work raising foreign money and wooing potential distributors among the minimajors. Both United Artists and Sony Pictures Classics showed interest.

The summer of 2003 dragged on. My anxiety level rose. Our

best shot to raise a budget, according to Alex, was at the Toronto Film Festival. He'd arranged several meetings there. One was with representatives of the South African government, another with the British financiers at Ingenious Film and Television. Three days later, Alex and our producer Hal Sadoff returned from Canada with the basis of a deal. They would raise the budget through a South African and British coproduction. The only problem was that South Africa and Britain didn't have a coproduction treaty, but Alex assured me he would make it work. All I wanted was to know when we could start.

I flew to L.A. and discussed dates with Cheadle. He was busy until Christmas 2003, then committed to *Ocean's Twelve* in early March 2004. Alex's best estimate of cash flow from the financiers was late November. That was too late. I insisted we needed to go into preproduction right away.

That night in Santa Monica, I bumped into Chris McGurk. The MGM vice-chairman told me he loved the script and that Cheadle was absolutely the right man for the role. He proved his commitment that same week by having UA commit to distribute.

We decided to go for a loan, get over to Africa, and prep for a 50-day shoot beginning January 3, 2004. If we shot all six-day weeks, we could make Cheadle's March 8 cutoff for *Ocean's Twelve*—if nothing went wrong.

On the way to Johannesburg, I stopped in London to meet with Sophie Okonedo (*Dirty Pretty Things*). I thought she'd be great for the role of Tatiana, but some of our backers were not so sure. I asked them to trust me.

In Johannesburg, we discovered that we'd picked the worse time of year to shoot a feature film. November through February is their commercial season; we were going to have problems getting a crew. I left Alex to sort out that problem. I called Sophie and told her she had the part. She asked me about a rehearsal schedule. "Forget it," I told her. We would have time for a quick cast read-through, some costume fittings, and then we'd go.

I set to work auditioning African actors and extras. We figured 10,000 over the course of the shoot. (It ballooned to 15,000.) The

Blid Alsbirk

Terry George, Don Cheadle, and Sophie Okonedo during shooting.

challenge was that many of these extras would have to act. The hotel staff extras had to behave like they'd been trained for a four-star establishment. The Hutu militia extras had to commit violence without overacting or hurting anyone. The children needed to look terrified. The white tourists only slightly less terrified. We assembled an even mix of South Africans, Rwandan and Burundian exiles, and Congolese immigrants. There was no common language; French was the most popular form of communication, Zulu and Swahili next, and finally English. I recruited six young theater directors from Soweto and Alexandra townships to help me. Some days, the grassy lawn behind the production offices resembled a madcap arts festival with marching militia, cowering refugees, and township children learning Rwandan dance steps.

In mid-October of 2003, the wheels started to come off our wagon. We lost our director of photography, Tom Sigel, to *The*

Brothers Grimm, which wouldn't finish on time. Our primary location on which to create Kigali's Mille Collines Hotel required a major refurbishment and wouldn't be ready when we needed it.

Worst of all, the financial deal was drowning in a sea of paperwork. In the meantime, Alex and I filled the gap with our own money, found a new DP (the great French cinematographer Robert Fraisse), and worked out a deal with the construction crews. They would take a week off only at Christmas, provided they got paid. By December 13, we were inundated with contracts, but the closing date for financing kept getting shifted by legal minutiae. Then, despite multiple promises that we would close the deal, the South African officials upped and went on vacation. Nothing would happen until at least January 6. We needed another loan, and more cash from Alex and myself, to keep going over the holiday period.

The New Year brought the reality that we would not sign off on January 6. We bit the bullet and moved the start date back a week. On the new schedule, we'd never make Don's cutoff date, but there was nothing to do but brave it out. Meanwhile, checks were bouncing harder than the summer rainstorms that battered the tin roofs of our hotel location. Alex assured me that all of the paper would be signed on January 7, allowing us to start the following week. Hal Sadoff spent 18 hours on the phone to make the deadline. At the last moment, the Industrial Development Corporation of South Africa demanded an amendment to one document—which required that 12 copies be faxed between L.A., London, Rome, and Johannesburg—and the time difference killed us. We couldn't close, we couldn't shoot. We had to push a day.

At 4 P.M. on Monday, January 12, the signature process began. Four hours later, we were financed. In total, we signed 97 documents, each requiring 12 signatures across three continents and ten time zones.

The next morning, I called "action." A mere four months had passed since Alex Ho had called from Toronto and said, "I think we can get the money, but it's complicated." Weeks later, the British government curtailed Ingenious Films' financing and shut down several other projects. We had made it by the skin of our teeth. Soon after shooting began, we learned that Brad Pitt had injured his Achilles tendon, thus forcing the postponement of *Ocean's Twelve.* Along the way, Joaquin Phoenix and Jean Reno both signed up for character roles. And some 15,000 South African, Rwandan, Burundian, and Congolese extras endured rain, mud, heat, and hail to help re-create the Rwandan genocide. I had fulfilled the first half of my promise: I had told the story. Now, we have to get the world to watch.

II.
Chronicles

Paul and Tatiana Rusesabagina

The Rwandan Schindler

Nicola Graydon

P aul Rusesabagina is, in most respects, unremarkable: a Rwandan of average height and stocky build, mild-mannered, polite and always impeccably dressed in dark suits and silk ties, he could easily be taken for a well-off businessman. But the former manager of the four-star Hotel des Mille Collines, in Kigali, is a great deal more than that. For 76 days in 1994 Rusesabagina acted as the Oscar Schindler of the Rwandan genocide. With little more than a well-stocked cellar, a single telephone line and a knack for persuasive banter, this self-effacing man—himself a Hutu of moderate political persuasion—kept the Hutu death squads away from the 1,268 terrified people who sought safety in his hotel. "Not one person was taken out, not one was beaten, not one was killed," he tells me. "That was my only concern—that no one should be harmed in my hotel."

That was not every Hutu's approach. In more obvious places of refuge—churches and schools, for instance—thousands upon

NICOLA GRAYDON is a journalist, broadcaster, and editor who contributes to various British publications including: *The Sunday Times Magazine*, *The Telegraph Magazine*, *The Mail on Sunday*, *The Daily Mail*, *The Evening Standard*, *Woman's Journal*, *Marie Claire*, and *Harpers and Queen*. Born in Johannesburg, she has traveled widely throughout Africa writing on issues from indigenous land rights to endangered species. In 2004, she traveled to Rwanda with Paul Rusesabagina on the 10th Anniversary of the 1994 genocide.

thousands were massacred. And many "respectable" Hutus carried out atrocities: businessmen, teachers, lawyers, clerics—all slaughtered their Tutsi compatriots, mostly with machetes and clubs. In just 100 days nearly a million were killed, among them some moderate Hutus. But it was primarily Tutsis who died; before the genocide, the Tutsi minority stood at more than 14 percent of the population; now it comprises just 9 percent.

It's no surprise, then, that to many Paul is a hero, one of very few people to emerge from the cataclysm with honor. His actions have brought him an international award, and his story is at the heart of *Hotel Rwanda*, a major new Hollywood film starring Don Cheadle as Paul, Nick Nolte as a hapless UN commander and Joaquin Phoenix as a journalist. The director, Terry George, says that he was captivated by the "shining example of humanity" that Rusesabagina displayed.

But Paul refuses to accept such praise, "What I did was normal," he insists. "When did the day arrive when not to kill is considered heroic? All I did was carry out my duties and responsibilities." Ten years after the genocide Paul has, briefly, come back to the Mille Collines. His feelings are mixed. In Brussels, where he's lived since 1996, it's easier to forget, but in Kigali the memories are raw: "Many of my friends turned into *genocidaires*. I was disappointed by them," he tells me, with typical understatement. "I used to think of them as gentlemen—correct and reasonable—and yet when it came to a mass massacre, they followed the mob. This, I will never understand."

Thankfully, Paul himself remained "correct and reasonable." The Mille Collines was the only sanctuary in the entire country where every single refugee survived the genocide—a murderous spree that had been planned for months and heralded by the hate spewed out from RTLMC, a radio station that was the mouthpiece of the Hutu Power movement. Such an outcome was all the more remarkable because many of the people in the hotel had been specifically targeted; in the Mille Collines were prominent Tutsi and Hutu politicians whose names were on lists

Frank Connor

Don Cheadle, as Paul Rusesabagina, negotiates with the Presidential Guard to protect his family and neighbors.

circulated to the death squads and read out on RTLMC. "They were like live bait," Major General Dallaire, the commander of the tiny UN peacekeeping force in Rwanda, recalls in his autobiography, "live bait being toyed with by a wild animal, at constant risk of being killed and eaten." Yet Dallaire could spare only four of his (unarmed) men to guard the hotel. The rest was left to Paul. How did he do it?

"I was acting systematically, like a thinking machine," he says. "It was only once I left the Mille Collines that I remembered it all like a nightmare."

Paul Rusesabagina's nightmare began on April 9, 1994, on the third day after the assassination of the Hutu President—an event used as the catalyst for the long-planned genocide to begin. Already, thousands had been slaughtered. And it was on that

The Mille Collines Hotel. The swimming-pool water at the Mille Collines Hotel was drunk by the refugees.

morning that members of the Presidential Guard arrived at Paul's home demanding that he take them to the Mille Collines' sister hotel, the Diplomates, which they wanted to use as their head-quarters.

Paul refused to leave without Tatiana, his Tutsi wife, their four children or a single one of the 32 neighbors sheltering in his living room, so they piled into a van and set off in convoy between two army jeeps. A mile down the road, the commanding officer stopped the convoy and handed Paul a Kalashnikov. "You're a traitor," the lieutenant said. "Take this gun, and kill these cock-roaches of yours." (Cockroach was the term extremist Hutus used to dehumanize their Tutsi victims.) Paul was, he tells me, sure he was going to die. The only question in his mind was whether he would be tempted to do the lieutenant's bidding and kill in order to save his family. "You must understand that killing was no longer a complicated thing," Paul explains. "We were surrounded by bodies. It was almost a joke, certainly it was normal." He pauses, and when he speaks again he is back in that moment when life and death hovered in the balance.

"'Listen, my friend,' I said to the gentleman. 'What interest do you have in killing that old man in the van? What will you gain? I know you people are hungry and tired. I can give you money. Why not negotiate?'" As Paul repeats the pleas he made then, he also repeats the pleading gestures he made, cupping his hands be-seechingly. "It didn't work: He said they were already being paid 200,000 francs for every Tutsi they killed. So I tried a different tack: 'If you want to kill them, go ahead,' I said. 'You won't profit. You won't gain anything. You are only 25 years old but you'll be liv-ing the whole of your life with blood on your hands.'" And then Paul said, in a phrase he would use again and again in the next months, "One day, all this will be over. How will you face history?" For close to an hour Paul negotiated until the Lieutenant accepted a deal. How much did he have to pay? "I never tell how much."

For Paul, it was a defining moment: "I felt I was already dead," he says. "But after that I always thought I would find a solution."

Fortunately, Paul was well-placed to find solutions. As in many African countries, the capital's leading hotel was the focal point around which the elite's social life took place. Inevitably Paul had met, and entertained, most of the country's leading political and military figures. He knew how business was done. Now the responsibility for doing the hotel's business devolved almost entirely on to him. Rwanda had been a Belgian colony; the Belgian airline Sabena had many interests there, including the Mille Collines and the Diplomates. When on April 11 almost the entire white community was evacuated, Paul's bosses among them, Paul was given control of Sabena's interests. The more politically connected in Kigali assumed that the Mille Collines—Sabena's crown jewel, and the location for press conferences given by General Dallaire—would be guarded by the UN. They flocked there hoping for a safe haven from the hideous slaughter that was taking place around them; by this stage, photographs taken by American spy satellites showed thousands of bodies floating down the Kagera River to Lake Victoria. By April 12 the 113-room hotel was running at full capacity: some 400 people had fled there. Over the next few days, the hotel began to resemble a refugee camp. "By the end we had 1,268 people," remembers Paul.

Paul saw it as his duty to protect them. His experience in dealing with the highest echelons of the Hutu military and political elite bore fruit. Deliberately, he courted them: "If you want to negotiate with someone, you need to keep them close, give them what they want," he says. What they wanted was alcohol, and they knew that Paul was in control of the finest cellars in town. Paul's attitude was pragmatic: "That's how things are done in Rwanda," he says, simply. "You talk, you negotiate, always over a drink." One of his more regular visitors was General Augustin Bizumungu, chief of staff of the army. Bizumungu is now serving a life sentence for crimes against humanity, but Paul will always be grateful to him for his help. Once the Interahamwe (Hutu militia) invaded the hotel, intent on killing the remaining Tutsi refugees. Paul was with Bizumungu at the Diplomates—stocks of beer and brandy at the Mille Collines had run out. He and Bizumungu rushed back to the Mille Collines; according to Paul, Bizumungu pulled his gun and started screaming, "If one person kills anyone, I will kill them; if anyone beats anyone, I will kill them; if you do not leave in five minutes, I will kill all of you." The Interahamwe left. During the genocide he needed men like Bizumungu: "For them, drinking cognac was a prestige thing, so was champagne, so that's what I gave them. This was my secret weapon."

So, while the condemned were encamped in the rooftop restaurant, Paul drank with the killers in the bars below.

Although the Mille Collines has a slightly run-down air today, it still boasts the best pool in Kigali—one in which children are, as we walk by, happily splashing. "This pool saved a lot of people," Paul remarks. "They cut off the water supply so people started drinking from it."

Inside the hotel, Zozo, the jocular concierge, greets Paul with immense warmth. Zozo, a Tutsi, is one of the few staff who remain from that terrible time: "Where else could I work?" he says. "The Mille Collines saved my life." He takes me to suite 261, which Paul and his family shared with two other families. "There were more than 40 people here," Zozo tells me. "But at least they had a room. New arrivals were coming in all the time. We couldn't turn them away. Finally, there were people everywhere: sleeping in the corridors, in the conference room—even in the cafeteria." The refugees were an extraordinary collection. The children of the murdered Tutsi prime minister, the former public prosecutor for Kigali and three subsequent prime ministers are all Mille Collines survivors. There were, too, priests and bishops, intellectuals, businessmen and journalists. Bizarrely, some *genocidaires* even brought their Tutsi wives and mothers, a factor that contributed to, though by no means guaranteed, the hotel's protection.

Zozo, a Tutsi and the concierge during the genocide, still works at the hotel: "The Mille Collines saved my life."

François Habiyakare, a moderate Hutu and former government minister, arrived with his wife and four children on the fourth day of the genocide: "There were people from every faction," he says. "Hutus, Tutsis, every political party—and yet all these people were living in complete harmony. And Paul was the reason: He was friendly with everybody, never showed favors whatever your status. If he had behaved differently, there could have been an internal war at the Mille Collines."

From the Peninsular, the swanky restaurant on the hotel's top floor, Paul could see the regular killings at the Church of the Holy Family in the valley below. He could also see piles of mutilated bodies lying in the streets, and the trucks that came every morning to collect them. But Paul had the living to worry about. He even bribed militia to fetch friends and colleagues of his. Odette and Jean Baptiste Gasasira, for example, are both doctors and well-known members of the Tutsi intelligentsia. The pair had attempted to flee Kigali with their children and with Odette's sister, a targeted parliamentarian. Attacked by a group of Hutus who shot and killed Odette's sister, they were forced to return home. There they heard their deaths announced on the radio.

They had been hiding in the bushes outside their house for two weeks before Paul finally reached them. He'd been ringing their house every night but Jean Baptiste had refused to let Odette answer—he feared it might be the militia checking to see if they were in fact still alive. "Finally Odette said, we either die of hunger, or we die by machete. Either way we die." She answered the phone. Jean Baptiste describes their arrival at the hotel in terms used by many Mille Collines survivors: "It was like walking from hell to an earthly paradise," he says. "And there were so many people there we thought had been killed. There was this strange comfort that we would die together. That's a bizarre thought, *non*? We were so happy because we would die with our friends."

Odette, who's now 52, sits under the banana tree in her garden, recalling daily life at the hotel: "There was mass every morning in the conference room on the fourth floor, followed by tea and porridge made with sorghum flour that Paul had managed to find, though mostly we lived on Air France airline meals that had been stored at the hotel. In the beginning we could have one each; by the end we had to split one between two. But all I could think about was the death of my sister. I heard the shot, I think I even heard her body fall, but I didn't even turn around. It haunted me."

There were joyful moments: Odette delivered a baby to a 17-year-old who was there with her boyfriend, a young Tutsi singer. The following week the couple were married by a resident bishop, and the baby was baptized. "We had bread for the first time in ages, so we really had a party," Odette remembers, with a wan smile. But François Habiyakare recalls an atmosphere of al-

Odette Nyiramilimo and Jean Baptiste Gasasira.
Below, actors Thulane Nyembe and Lebo Mashile
portray Jean Baptiste and Odette in *Hotel Rwanda*.

Gianluigi Guercia

Blid Alsbirk

most constant fear. "For weeks we waited to die. The militia attacked us several times and towards the end we were also shelled. And there was the possibility we could die of hunger."

The days were punctuated by new arrivals. "Then it was always emotional," says Odette. "We would be so happy they were alive but they all brought terrible stories of what had happened to their families and ours. Then we cried with them." But even in the darkness, there was decency. Odette remembers the arrival of a man riven with anguish about his pregnant wife. The couple had been forced out of hiding when she went into labour. When soldiers came into view, she had been unable to flee; he had watched from the bushes as the soldiers led her away. He was convinced they had killed her. A week later she arrived at the Mille Collines with their baby on her back.

"It was incredible," says Odette. "The soldiers had taken her to hospital and then she walked back through all the roadblocks telling everyone she was going to the father of her child. For some reason they let her through. There were some miracles like that. Stories that made you believe God had not deserted us entirely." Jean Baptiste interrupts: "The hand of God was everywhere. Of course, Paul helped. Maybe that was it. Maybe Paul wasn't an employee of Sabena at all, maybe he was working for God." At that the two friends laugh long and loud.

Early on, negotiations began to allow hotel residents to be evacuated to Tutsi-held areas. Most of those in the Mille Collines assumed Paul would leave as soon as possible, as they would have done. Instead he decided to stay until the last of the guests had been taken to safety. Unaware of this, a group of refugees approached Paul and told him "they didn't want to be killed with machetes; they said they were going to throw themselves from the roof, to die honourably without being cut to pieces; they wanted permission to do that in my hotel. When I told them I was staying, they took me for a madman." So did Tatiana and Jean Baptiste, who were among the first to attempt evacuation; they tried to persuade Paul to leave, but he was adamant. "Convincing them wasn't easy," he says. "I told them, 'If I save my own life, what will it be like to remember that over 1,000 people died in this place because of me? How would I face history?'"

The first attempted evacuation, on May 3, went badly wrong. Seventy people—including Paul's family and the Gasasiras—were in the convoy, but someone alerted the RTLMC. The convoy was stopped and the refugees were badly beaten. It was not until May 27 that safe passage could be secured for a group of more than 100 refugees. The night before the evacuation the families gathered in suite 261 and made a pact. "We decided that whoever lived would take care of the children as if they were their own," says Jean Baptiste. "And we told the children they were now blood brothers and sisters." The next day they were loaded on trucks and driven, safely, to a Tutsi-held zone. The hotel was finally evacuated on June 18 without the loss of a single life.

Liberation proved a mixed blessing. Paul and Tatiana drove south towards Tatiana's childhood home, in good times a leisurely drive over rolling hills and through villages teeming with life. Now the countryside was silent. "There were no people, no cars, no animals. The only sound was the noise of dogs eating the rotting bodies. The whole country smelled of death." At the house a trail of blood led from the living room to a mass grave. There they found the bodies of Tatiana's mother, sister-in-law, six grandsons and a granddaughter. Paul felt a surge of anger: "If I had had a gun at that moment, I could have killed someone." It was the first emotion he had given way to in weeks.

Paul carried on running the Hotel des Mille Collines for nearly two years. Though the immediate catalyst for his self-exile in 1996 was an attack on his home by a Tutsi soldier, one senses his reasons for departure lie in a deeper despair at his country's situation. A proposal, for instance, to honor the Hutus who risked their lives to save their Tutsi compatriots was blocked by the current Tutsi-dominated government, and the idea of throwing a Mille Collines anniversary celebration also foundered on political grounds.

Paul shrugs. "I have always been in opposition," he says. "And I hate to keep my mouth shut. But we Rwandans still refuse to call evil by its own name. It is always to do with 'the other.' The Hutus will tell you a history that favors their side; the Tutsis do the same. To me, we are all guilty. I lost members of my family to both ideologies. We need to sit around a table together—Hutus and Tutsis—and negotiate the future."

Indeed. For, as Paul Rusesabagina told the murderous militia, "One day all this will be over. How will you face history?"

Paul and Tatiana Rusesabagina, above, and below, as portrayed by Sophie Okonedo and Don Cheadle in the film *Hotel Rwanda*.

The Struggle of Memory Against Forgetting

Anne Thompson

"The struggle of man against power is the struggle of
memory against forgetting."
—Milan Kundera, *The Book of Laughter and Forgetting*

Terry George's *Hotel Rwanda* belongs to that honorable
Hollywood tradition from *The Killing Fields* to *The Pianist*:
Take horrifying events in the world, show audiences how
and why they happened, and remind them not to repeat history.

A Northern Irishman, George has a talent for taking tough-to-
dramatize stories and bringing them to the screen. He wrote the
Oscar-nominated *In the Name of the Father* and *The Boxer* for his
friend, director Jim Sheridan. He made his directing debut with
Some Mother's Son, a wrenching drama about the 1980's hunger
strikes staged by Northern Irish women whose sons were impris-
oned by the British Army.

ANNE THOMPSON is the Deputy Film Editor of *The Hollywood Reporter*
and a regular contributor to *Premiere, Wired, Filmmaker, New York Magazine, The New York Times, The Washington Post*, and *The London Observer*.
From 1996 to 2002, she headed *Premiere*'s Los Angeles bureau as West
Coast Editor. Before joining *Premiere*, she was a senior writer at *Entertainment Weekly* and West Coast Editor at *Film Comment Magazine*, and
she wrote the film industry column "Risky Business" for *L.A. Weekly*
and *The Los Angeles Times Syndicate*.

Now he was tackling an African story set against the genocide of nearly a million people. How was he going to dramatize that? Soften it too much, and it loses authenticity. Go too far with the horror, and you risk making audiences run for the exits. So George turned *Hotel Rwanda* into a love story about a husband and wife who not only do everything they can to protect their own family, but try to save as many people as they can from certain death.

Like many Americans, I had been only dimly aware of the real dimensions of what had happened during those months of terror in 1994. The West didn't pay more attention to the genocide partly because the media that rarely devotes time to serious coverage of Africa anyway was focused at the time on the end of apartheid rule in South Africa. Until I read Terry George and Keir Pearson's script, I had never read about hotel manager Paul Rusesabagina's heroic acts during the Rwandan genocide ten years ago.

Without resorting to a narrator or flashbacks, George and Pearson's script lays out the information that a viewer needs to know about a complex situation. In the simplest terms, when Belgium and Holland, respectively, took over Rwanda and South Africa in 1918, in order to rule the majority native population, they introduced different ways of viewing, measuring, demeaning, and subjugating the people. In the case of Rwanda, the Belgians at first chose the dominant Tutsi tribes, who were land-owning herders, to be their managerial ruling class, because they were supposedly more "European"-looking, with thinner lips and noses and finer hair. They handed out ID cards to every citizen classifying them as Tutsi or Hutu—although they had been inter-marrying for generations. Eventually the Belgians withdrew in 1961-62, and when the Hutus, who were farmers working under feudal Tutsi overlords, inevitably rose up and overthrew their op-pressors, they imposed their own pattern of ethnic abuse. In April 1994, during a government turnover, Hutu death squads massa-cred the Tutsis by the thousands. This slaughter went on day after day, week after week, for 100 days, until an estimated 800,000 Tutsis along with nearly 200,000 Hutu supporters had been killed.

The United Nations, America, France, Belgium, and the rest of the world saw it coming, stood by, and did nothing.

When United Artists sends me George's script and offers me the chance to cover the filming of Hotel Rwanda on location in South Africa, I jump at the chance. After fifteen hours in the air, when my plane lands in Johannesburg, I am thrilled to be visiting Africa for the first time. It's February 2004, JoBurg's spring, rainy season. A lanky production driver meets me at the airport and hugs me enthusiastically. "I'm Albert," he says. It's tough to penetrate his guttural accent. Like many South African citizens, Albert speaks seven of the eleven official languages, including English, Afrikaner, Zulu, and his native Zutu.

We drive in a scuffed white van through the city to an abandoned convention center in a suburb about a half hour away from the airport, which provides production offices as well as a constructed replica of the Mille Collines Hotel in Kigali, the capital of Rwanda, where Paul Rusesabagina had harbored some 1,200 refugees. Producer Alex Kitman Ho, a veteran of several Oliver Stone movies including *Platoon*, shows me some chilling early footage on his portable computer. "We must cut the tall trees now," barks a Hutu radio announcer. "Wipe out these Tutsi cockroaches."

Ho feels strongly that the filmmakers chose the right approach in not casting stars like Denzel Washington, Will Smith, or Halle Berry. "It's a totally different movie with Denzel as the hero," says Ho. "You know he's going to succeed at the end. Part of the magic is you don't know what's going to happen."

So Ho and George lined up a strong international cast willing to cut their salaries for the project: Don Cheadle (*Traffic*), Sophie Okonedo (*Dirty Pretty Things*), Nick Nolte (*Prince of Tides*), Joaquin Phoenix (*Signs*), and Jean Reno (*Fifth Element*). "We got lucky," says Ho. "We cobbled together global financing for a $17-million budget, a third in South Africa." The money saved on big stars went into hiring some 12,000 extras, as many as 950 a day, to show the scale of the drama. "[More than] 800,000 people died," says

Blid Alsbirk

South African locals, some of whom are Tutsi refugees, were hired as extras. This scene depicts the terror taking place outside the walls of the Mille Collines.

Ho. "You have to see some of them. It's about a massacre."

Extras dressed as soldiers, diplomats, and assorted hotel guests are milling about on the lawn by the pool behind the Mille Collines set. It's a campsite littered with tables, mattresses, wash tubs, umbrellas, plastic clotheslines, makeshift tents made out of garbage bags, turned-over resort chairs, teepees, cardboard and bamboo mats. It's raining into the swimming pool. A set decorator is spraying blankets to make them look dirty.

"Some of the extras are locals, some are Tutsi refugees," explains unit publicist Stephen Maresch on the set. "Reenacting what they went through has not been easy. Some are still fearful of men dressed like Rwandan guards. Ten years ago, they were real."

Crammed inside the hotel bar interior, Terry George, a ruddy-faced tall man in a floppy hat, is shooting a scene with a

Blid Alsbirk

Joaquin Phoenix, as Jack, questions Chloe, played by Noxolo Maqashalala, about the difference between Tutsis and Hutus.

bearded Joaquin Phoenix as a TV cameraman talking to a journalist and two young women.

"What's the difference between a Hutu and a Tutsi?" Phoenix asks.

"According to Belgian colonists, Tutsis were taller and more elegant," says the journalist. "They picked people—with thinner noses, lighter skin, they used to measure the width of their noses—to run the country for them."

"Get out of here," says Phoenix. He turns flirtatiously to one of the girls.

"What are you, Hutu?"

"Tutsi," she says.

"They could be twins," he says.

After they complete the shot, George and I grab some chairs

before the next set-up. He compares the film to *"The Killing Fields*, about an ordinary man who triumphs over enormous evil," he says, with a slight Irish lilt. "This is *Schindler's List* for Africa. The Mille Collines is like *Casablanca*. Society in turmoil, gunrunners, tourists, intelligence agents all mixed in. I wanted it to be a love story and a political thriller about an ordinary man who finds the courage he never thought he had, and with each step manages to hold off an army."

George explains that Paul Rusesabagina, who was Hutu, was able to take advantage of his myriad relationships across Rwandan society. "He uses his skills dealing with people," George says. "His charm, ability to bargain, a great reservoir of common sense: 'Please accept money for these people, they are worthless to you.' Behind that there was a deep commitment to his family—which he was forced to extend to an ever-growing family. He had to overcome fear, while managing to hold a lot of disparate tensions at bay."

The movie shouldn't dwell on the bloodshed, George feels. "The whole gore factor didn't interest me in the slightest," he says. "I wanted people to feel a love story and an individual story rather than a docudrama about a massacre. I wanted to give more of a sense of the fear and craziness of it, an epic story shot in classic style told through the eyes of this man. This story needs to be chronicled, it's one of the great acts of heroism of the twentieth century."

We move through the broad, blond-wood lobby and out the glass front doors of the hotel. Militiamen are lolling on the grass near a line of fake palm trees. George goes over to Don Cheadle, standing in the hotel forecourt, wearing a natty blue suit, shiny black shoes, blue shirt, and red tie, joking with Joaquin Phoenix, who is hoisting a video camera, and a clean-shaven Nick Nolte, sporting a blue beret as the UN's Colonel Oliver. In the circular driveway a line of UN peacekeepers in muddy boots and blue helmets lean against a UN truck, holding automatic rifles.

A camera assistant slaps the clapboard in front of the camera. "Rolling!" calls the camera operator. "Sound!" cries the sound mixer. "And action!" yells George. He slouches in his director's

Sophie Okonedo, the children, and Nick Nolte greet Paul Rusesabagina, center, on the set.

chair behind a video playback monitor, wearing headphones. The set is hushed.

"We are not allowed to interfere," Nolte tells Cheadle, as he escorts the finance minister into the hotel, a boom mike bobbing over his head.

"I have more refugees than I have room for as it is," Cheadle replies.

"As soon as I can stabilize the situation, then I'll take them."

Nolte's role is several generals and colonels rolled into one, but he is modeling his character mainly on French Canadian Lieutenant General Roméo Dallaire, author of *Shake Hands with the Devil*. "He journaled everything," says Nolte, sitting in his director's chair. "Some say that he could have stopped it. He didn't defy orders. It would have been a brave thing to do, if there had been a stronger guy there. He could have been court-martialed."

Nolte shakes his head as he remembers his meeting with Rusesabagina. "Paul took me aside and tried to communicate to me," he says. "His eyes. There just aren't words for it. I asked him, 'Did you ever feel fear?' He said, 'There was no time for fear. Every time I turned around I had to make a decision.'"

Don Cheadle and I sit inside the quiet lobby on a brown leather sofa. At 40, Cheadle has earned the status of an in-demand, internationally known actor of remarkable range. He has four movies coming out this year: *Ocean's Twelve*, *The Assassination of Richard Nixon*, *After the Sunset*, and *Tishomingo Blues*, which he directed. Despite his crazy schedule, because it is so tough to get an African story made, Cheadle attached his name to *Hotel Rwanda* early on to help get the movie financed. "Rwanda was an incredibly under-reported, under-noticed event in the world's history," he says. "This is a real great example of how fear caught up with prejudice, how all these things intermingle in the worst way. Human beings in the proper setting will do things that are unimaginable. The film's conclusion is absolutely positive: you see love triumph over everything, how man's purity can still find humanity, it is possible. When everything is pulled out from under you, what else is there? That's all we have at the end of the day."

Cheadle was able to sit down with Rusesabagina over several meals. "There were so many things I wanted to ask him about," he says. "I was hesitant to ask him to dredge up horrific things. I was always very careful. He saw piles of bodies; his wife lost hundreds in her family. I didn't want to push him. He had to bring all his tools to bear on this situation that was not knowingly premeditated, and he was like a duck to water."

After weeks of 13-hour days, Cheadle admits, "I feel a good exhaustion at the end of the day. It's a great workout. Terry hired me to know Paul. I'm always insecure and intimidated, but I trust Terry. He's a great writer. He always goes back to the story."

Outside on the lawn, one striking Tutsi actor, who has been liv-

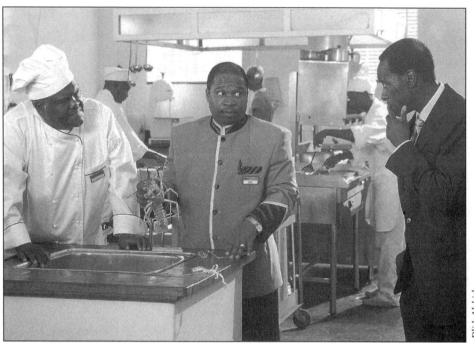

Renowned South African comedian Desmond Dube, center, plays a hotel porter.

ing in South Africa with his second wife and two kids for five years, describes how Tutsis seeking sanctuary filled Catholic churches in Rwanda, only to be mowed down by the thousands by militia extremists. "Sixty people in my family were killed," he says, his eyes burning. "[In 1994 I was with my] first wife [who] was Hutu. She was hiding, had to separate from me, she was pregnant, and her family made her have an abortion."

When he first came on set and met Rusesabagina, who was famed in Rwanda for his actions, "I cried," he says. "It made me remember how he behaved. I thanked him for what he did. He didn't know I went to my trailer to wash my face. Why didn't other people behave like him? When people ask me what I am doing here, it's because I want to show an example of what really happened in Rwanda."

For the extras, participating in the film was cathartic, Cheadle says. "On set, one of the Rwandan extras playing a militia guy was a Hutu, and he was threatening people. They had to pay him to leave. There are people here with machete scars, rape victims. It was important for them to participate and support this movie. They feel like their story was never sufficiently documented or told to the world."

We are joined by Desmond Dube, the star of a comedy variety TV show in South Africa, who plays Rusesabagina's unflappable second-in-command, named Dube. "When we first started shooting, I was a bit afraid of a white man telling a black story," he says. "If people see it as too light, you could criticize him for being insensitive. But Terry doesn't want audiences to see a horror movie. He's trying to keep it not too bloody."

When Rusesabagina visited the set, they were filming a scene when many people, including Paul's Tutsi wife, Tatiana, and his children, try to leave the hotel in a convoy of UN trucks and fall into an ambush from Hutu death squads wielding machetes. "Somebody asked Paul his opinion of the shot," says Dube. "'There isn't enough blood,'" he said. "'When the people opened the truck, all they could see was blood before they could see the people.'"

Rusesabagina's son Roger, a round-faced, sad-eyed 25-year-old studying hotel management at the University of Michigan, was on that convoy too. He was 15, and "200 people were lined up to kill you, that was the most harrowing," says Roger. "After that I wanted to stay in the hotel and not leave. We were smuggled out to an RPF [Rwanda Patriotic Front, the opposition force] place two weeks later."

Being on the set isn't real to him. "This is fun," he says. "The situation then scared me. Now I am laughing. The place didn't look like this exactly. While it's happening, you don't think about being scared anymore, but you've lost all your friends, they've died. You're locked up in a hotel with people waiting to kill you and no idea if you're going to die. You just try to live every day like it's your last. If someone was going to die, my dad would die first because he was in front of all of us."

Frank Connor

Don Cheadle, left, with Paul Rusesabagina.

* * *

In the fall, *Hotel Rwanda* debuts at the Toronto Film Festival. Paul Rusesabagina is there when the crowd rises to give him a rousing standing ovation. It's no surprise when the film wins the Audience Award. And goes on to win the same award at the AFI Fest in Los Angeles. In November, George and Rusesabagina come to speak after a well-attended screening of the movie for my Sneak Previews class at UCLA's Wadsworth Theater. As Rusesabagina walks down the aisle, 900 film-loving adult West Siders rise to their feet and applaud. Many are moved to tears.

Sitting behind microphones on stage, George is still passionate about challenging the world to pay attention to what happened ten years ago—and the genocide that is still ongoing in Darfur. "Rwanda came two months after the battles in Somalia, *Black Hawk Down*," he explains. "The ineffectiveness of the UN led to their reluctance to get involved. Hutu extremists knew that if they killed a certain amount of western soldiers—they killed ten—they would leave. They waged a deliberate campaign blocking intervention."

"Human life in Africa isn't worth the same as a man's life anywhere else is," adds George. "What happens in one place can come home to roost in another."

What would it have taken to stop the killing? "The Santa Monica police force could have come down and saved those people," George states flatly. "It was not like Somalia, not an Islamic jihad with the country armed to the teeth. The bulk of the country was running around with machetes. The radio was a vital character in the film, to see the extent that hate radio can go, when you start demonizing people like that. They become cockroaches to be wiped out."

What did you think of Don Cheadle? Rusesabagina, a charismatic, well-spoken man with a contained power, charms the crowd when he says, "I talked with Don so that he could see who I was. He watched my manners. He picked up both my good and my bad manners."

How did you feel on the set, reliving your past? "I stayed fifteen days on the shoot. Whenever I saw something that happened in 1994 it was always something reopening the wounds, wakening up the old demons. What happened you could not put up on the screen. But I appreciate what Terry did."

The audience applauds enthusiastically. George wants as many people as possible to see the movie, and thus fought the MPAA's initial R rating. "We had a hearing before the board," he says. "The woman said, 'You can't have a film where you see a van running over dead bodies.' You don't see. It was in her own head. We got a PG-13."

He exhorts the crowd to help *Hotel Rwanda:* "We depend on word-of-mouth to spread the word on this movie."

On their way out of the theater, George and Rusesabagina are surrounded by well-wishers thanking them and asking how they can help. George refers them to HotelRwanda.com for more information on what they can do.

Outside the theatre, one well-coiffed woman turns to her friend. "I would never have gone to see this movie," she says. "I'm glad I did."

Bill Clinton (left) and Pasteur Bizimungo, the then-President of Rwanda, at a press conference on March 25, 1998, where Clinton came "to pay the respects of my nation to all who suffered and all who perished in the Rwandan genocide."

FRONTLINE / PBS
The Triumph of Evil

Narrator: In March 1998, as the Monica Lewinsky scandal was consuming his presidency, Bill Clinton escaped to Africa, to make his long-planned tour of the continent. He had come to offer hope, to strengthen America's commitment to Africa, and on this afternoon in Kigali, the capital of Rwanda, he had come to apologize.

Pres. Bill Clinton: I have come today to pay the respects of my nation to all who suffered and all who perished in the Rwandan genocide.

Narrator: The genocide five years ago in Rwanda was meticulously planned and brutally executed, the methodical slaughter of over 800,000 Tutsis and their sympathizers.

Philip Gourevitch, *The New Yorker*: There have been cases of mass political murder, but never a country and a society so completely and totally convulsed by an effort at pure, unambiguous genocide since the end of World War II, and the world left the Rwandans to it.

This FRONTLINE/PBS documentary originally aired on January 26, 1999. It was produced by Mike Robinson, Ben Loeterman; reported on by Steve Bradshaw; and written by Steve Bradshaw and Ben Loeterman.

Narrator: The killing lasted 100 days, sometimes over 10,000 killed each day. All the while America—and the world—did almost nothing to stop it.

James Woods, Deputy Asst. Secretary of Defense, 1986-94: People didn't want to really grasp and admit that they knew and understood what was happening because they didn't want to bear the consequences then of dealing with it. They did not want an intervention.

Pres. Bill Clinton: It may seem strange to you here, especially the many of you who lost members of your family, but all over the world there were people like me sitting in offices, day after day after day, who did not fully appreciate the depth and the speed with which you were being engulfed by this unimaginable terror.

Narrator: The story behind President Clinton's dramatic apology for the world's failure in Rwanda is a story about the triumph of evil, which the philosopher Edmund Burke observed happens when good men do nothing.

Michael Barnett, U.S. Mission to the UN, 1994: What really haunts me was that I and others could have been so cavalier, so complacent.

Interviewer: Do you believe that you were a bystander to genocide?

Michael Barnett: Yeah. We all were.

Narrator: In April, 1993, during the first months of his new administration, President Clinton officially dedicated the new Holocaust Museum in Washington.

Pres. Bill Clinton: To preserve this shared history of anguish, to keep it vivid and real so that evil can be combated and contained, we are here to consecrate this memorial and to contemplate its meaning for us.

Blid Alsbirk

Jack, a journalist played by Joaquin Phoenix, predicts that despite the reports that he and his colleagues are broadcasting, "people will go on eating their dinners."

The evil represented in this museum is incontestable, but as we are its witness, so must we remain its adversary in the world in which we live.

Narrator: The discovery of the Nazi death camps 50 years earlier had shocked the world into bold new promises, a universal Declaration of Human Rights and the United Nations genocide convention that pledged the world would never again tolerate attempts to exterminate whole groups of people.

Pres. Bill Clinton: Our task, with God's blessing upon our souls and the memories of the fallen in our hearts and minds, is to the ceaseless struggle to preserve human rights and dignity. I pray that we shall prevail.

Narrator: As the President added his voice to the ritual chorus of "never again," his new administration was formulating its foreign policy and making hard-nosed decisions about where America's interests really lay.

James Woods, Deputy Asst. Secretary of Defense, 1986-94: In the Spring of '93, when the Clinton administration came in, we were asked to develop lists of what we thought would be serious crises this administration might face and forward that to the new secretary of defense, Mr. Aspin. I put Rwanda-Burundi on the list.

I won't go into personalities, but I received guidance from higher authorities, "Look, if something happens in Rwanda-Burundi, we don't care. Take it off the list. It's not—U.S. national interest is not involved and," you know, "we can't put all these silly humanitarian issues on lists like important problems like the Middle East and North Korea and so on."

Narrator: In 1993, Rwanda, one of Africa's smallest countries with just seven million citizens, was a deeply troubled country with a deeply troubled past. Decades earlier, under colonial rule, the Belgians had used the Tutsis, Rwanda's aristocracy, to enforce their rule over the Hutu majority, who were mostly poor farmers.

Philip Gourevitch, *The New Yorker*: The Belgians created an idea whereby the Tutsi were a master race, the Hutu an inferior race. And ethnic identity cards were issued. Much like in South Africa, an apartheid-like system was imposed. All privileges went to the Tutsi minority, and the Hutu majority was almost in bondage.

At independence in the late '50s and early '60s, this system was reversed. The majority Hutu rebelled, seized power, in the name of majority rule imposed an apartheid-like system in reverse and oppressed the Tutsi bitterly.

Narrator: Faced with discrimination and increasing Hutu violence, most Tutsis fled to neighboring countries, where they formed a guerrilla army, the Rwandan Patriotic Front.

In 1990, the rebel Tutsis invaded Rwanda and forced peace talks with Juvenal Habyarimana, the Hutu president. Anxious to

Rwandan Patriotic Front leader Paul Kagame, who became President of Rwanda in 2000, tours a rural area with his troops in February 1993.

stay in power himself, Habyarimana signed a peace treaty agreeing to share power with the Tutsis.

Philip Gourevitch: To the Hutu extremists who formed the entourage around the Hutu dictatorship, President Habyarimana, it was the threat of peace that was even greater than the threat of war because it amounted to a defeat. It meant that they couldn't have a total victory. They faced suddenly the threat of sharing power, which was the one thing on earth that they couldn't stand sharing.

Narrator: Late in 1993, the United Nations dispatched its Assistance Mission for Rwanda—or UNAMIR—to help keep the fragile new peace between the Hutu government and the Tutsi rebels. The UN force was small, about 2,500 soldiers from several countries, including Belgium and Ghana. In the beginning they had believed this would be a routine peacekeeping mission.

Brig. Henry Anyidoho, Deputy Commander, UNAMIR: From all the indications, because I had served on some other UN missions before, but at first the level of 2,548 indicated clearly that it was going to be an easy mission, or it was anticipated to be an easy mission.

Narrator: But the UN troops would have to contend with Hutu extremists and their militias—the Interahamwe—literally "those who attack together." They claimed their mission was simply to defend Rwanda from the Tutsi guerrillas. But in January, 1994, the man training them came forward with a very different story.

Col. Luc Marchal, UNAMIR: Yes, he was a real political leader for the militia, and he wants to give us, I mean to UNAMIR, some information. I met him in my own headquarters. It was at night. There was no electricity.

Narrator: In that secret meeting, the Hutu informant revealed that the militia's real mission was the extermination of the Tutsis.

Col. Luc Marchal: So the directive was very simple. Just kill a maximum of people.

Interviewer: "People" meaning civilians?

Col. Luc Marchal: Yes, of course, civilians. Tutsis, of course.

Narrator: Later that night, the UNAMIR commanders sent an urgent message to the peacekeeping mission at the United Nations in New York. Their coded cable explained the Hutu informant's warning in horrifying detail.

Cable: "He has been ordered to register all Tutsi in Kigali. He suspects it's for their extermination. Example he gave was that in 20 minutes his personnel could kill up to 1,000 Tutsis."

Rwandan force commander Roméo Dallaire, left, with UN envoy Igbal Riza, right, on May 26, 1994, in Kigali, Rwanda.

Iqbal Riza, Chief of Staff to UN Secretary General: It alarmed us. It alarmed us that people are being targeted, that this particular person is training people. It was alarming.

Narrator: The UN commanders in Rwanda wanted to act fast to foil the Interahamwe. In the cable to New York, UNAMIR said it planned to seize some of the militias weapons.

Interviewer: When you read that the force commander wanted to go on an arms raid, how did you react?

Iqbal Riza: We said, "Not Somalia again."

Narrator: This was the UN's nightmare, pictures of 18 American Rangers killed in Somalia on primetime T.V. They had died after a raid like the one UNAMIR was now proposing in Rwanda. The

UN had taken the blame and wasn't going to risk another bloody African adventure.

So late the same night, the UN's bureaucrats in New York warned UNAMIR its plan to seize weapons was not what UN peacekeepers should be doing. The cable was sent under the name of Kofi Annan, then head of UN peacekeeping and now secretary general. It was signed by his colleague, Iqbal Riza, now his chief of staff. It told UNAMIR to avoid actions that might lead to the use of force and unanticipated repercussions. It said, "We cannot agree to the operation."

Col. Luc Marchal, UNAMIR: We knew that a lot of weapons were hidden in caches. And we were not authorized, I should say, to do our job, and that was a real frustration.

Iqbal Riza: We did not give that information the importance and the correct interpretation that it deserved. We realized that only in hindsight. I'm not denying that.

Interviewer: It was a mistake?

Iqbal Riza: Oh, certainly. We—we—

Interviewer: Was it a mistake that cost lives, do you believe?

Iqbal Riza: Eventually, yes, three months later.

Narrator: Three months later, April 6, 1994. It had been a year since President Clinton dedicated the Holocaust Museum. At the Capitol, Vice President Al Gore was speaking about its continuing meaning for Americans.

Vice Pres. Al Gore: The Holocaust is not an event to be remembered just by those who survived, or just by Jews or just by gypsies. Its memorial should continue to be part of the American experience for everyone. And there is no better place for it than Washington, to remind those who make the agonizing decisions of foreign policy of the consequences of those decisions.

Narrator: Later that night in Africa, President Habyarimana of Rwanda was flying back to Kigali with the President of Burundi after more peace talks with the Tutsis. It was to be their last flight.

Peter Jennings, ABC News: *["World News Now"]* In Africa today, a plane carrying the presidents of two African countries has apparently been shot down as it was coming in for a landing in the capital of Rwanda. UN officials say both presidents were killed.

Narrator: The President's plane had been shot down by missiles. Nobody knows who fired them.

In the power vacuum that followed, the Hutu extremists seized their chance. The plan the informant had warned about three months earlier now began to unfold. The militias set up roadblocks and began to look for Tutsis—men, women and children.

Brig. Henry Anyidoho, Deputy Commander, UNAMIR: I couldn't believe it. You met men and women together at the roadblocks holding the cutlasses, or machetes as, they call them, and all of them sort of, like—they were singing war songs. And what were they looking for? Human beings to hack to death.

Narrator: National radio acted as a cheerleader for the slaughter. The Tutsis, it said, must become nothing but a memory.

Philip Gourevitch, *The New Yorker:* Following the president's death, it became almost "genocide central." It was through there that people were instructed at times, "Go out there and kill. You must do your work. People are needed over in this commune."

Sometimes they actually had disc jockeys who would direct—they would say, "So-and-So has just fled. He is said to be moving down such-and-such a street." And they would literally hunt an individual who was targeted, in the streets, and people would listen to this on the radio. It was apparently quite dramatic.

Narrator: Within 24 hours the UN's camps had begun to shelter

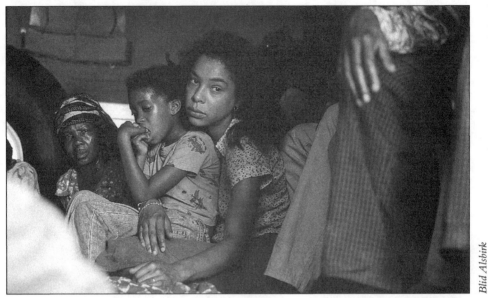

Tatiana, played by Sophie Okonedo, on the crowded UN convoy. Moments later the truck is intercepted by Hutu militia who have been notified of their whereabouts by radio reports.

terrified civilians. Some fled to a school called Don Bosco, where the largest Belgian contingent was digging in. They were ordinary families running from their neighbors. The commanding officer, Captain Lemaire, had no doubts about the danger they were facing.

Capt. Luc Lemaire, UNAMIR: From the first hours, I knew there was a risk. We've heard a lot of explosion in the direct neighborhoods and we realized immediately that they were murdering people all around Don Bosco.

Narrator: Everyone who fled to the school had a tale of horror.

Florida Ngulinzira: *[through interpreter]* We even saw children, very small children, three-year-olds, four-year-olds arriving at the school saying, "Mummy and Daddy have been killed. They've been killed with machetes."

Narrator: Some killers even infiltrated the camp, but were captured by the Belgians. Outside Don Bosco, the UN troops could only watch as cavalcades of killers armed with machetes, guns and grenades cruised by triumphantly.

Capt. Luc Lemaire: They used to massacre people in one part of the commune, and afterwards they went away to find other people to massacre.

Narrator: But UNAMIR wasn't just protecting civilians from the killers, it was also guarding the moderate politicians who stood in their way. In secret cables, UNAMIR intelligence officers had warned the moderates, too, were in danger. This memo detailed a murder plot against a leading politician called Lando.

But when the killers came for Lando, his outnumbered UN guards stood aside. Trapped in his house with his family, he made a series of increasingly desperate phone calls.

Nausicaa Habimana, Lando's Niece: *[through interpreter]* He told my mother that this was the end, that he was going to die, and he said good-bye. And when my mother put the phone down, she told us that Lando was going to die. That was all she said.

Narrator: Lando and his Canadian wife made one last call to UN headquarters, pleading with the local commander to send more troops.

Col. Luc Marchal, UNAMIR: He was like his wife, he was desperate. At a certain moment, I heard explosions of hand grenades, shooting of arms, and Mr. Lando said, "It's too late," and it was the last word of Mr. Lando.

Narrator: The bodies of Lando, his wife and four other members of their family were found in the ruins of their house. In the first few days, at least another 18 moderate leaders were murdered. Lando's Ghanaian body guards disappeared for a day, but finally turned up unharmed.

Interviewer: Your men were there to protect Mr. Lando—

Brig. Henry Anyidoho: Yes.

Interviewer: —and his family. Do you think you let him down?

Brig. Henry Anyidoho: In a sense, Mr. Lando, if he were to be alive, or any of his relations, will feel that the UN let him down. But I think the force that we put there did what was expected of them.

Narrator: Not only did the UN fail to protect the politicians, some of its troops were unable to protect themselves. Ten Belgian soldiers were tricked into giving up their weapons only to be attacked by an angry mob. The soldiers were tortured and horribly mutilated before they were killed. It was all part of a strategy.

Philip Gourevitch, *The New Yorker*: The Rwandans who were planning a genocide, the Hutu extremists around the president, they said, "Look, if we kill some of them, they'll go away." That was in the fax that was sent to UN headquarters. It was predicted that they were planning to kill some Belgians. And sure enough, on the morning after the president's assassination, they killed these blue helmets.

Capt. Luc Lemaire: My men were horrified because they thought it should have been an easy mission and they suddenly discovered it was a nightmare.

Interviewer: And was your reaction immediately to think, "We must get out of Rwanda"?

Capt. Luc Lemaire: Certainly not, because as soldiers we have to be ready to die at any moment.

Narrator: But in Belgium, the shocked government was planning to pull all its troops out of Rwanda. In a secret attempt to save face, its foreign ministry lobbied countries on the Security Council, asking them to vote to withdraw the whole UN force.

Karel Kovanda, Czech UN Ambassador, 1994: I recall getting a phone call from a colleague of mine in Prague, who got a call from the Belgium foreign minister lobbying him, or lobbying the Czech Republic through him, that we should act to pull UN-AMIR out of Rwanda.

Interviewer: So they were even phoning up civil servants in foreign capitals—

Karel Kovanda: Well, they were—

Interviewer: —saying, "Let's all get out."

Karel Kovanda: They were—well, my sense is that they were phoning the ranking officer of every foreign service—of every foreign ministry of the 15 countries.

Interviewer: Is this normal?

Karel Kovanda: Oh, I would say that it's highly unusual. I have never heard anything of the sort before.

Narrator: In Washington American officials were only too ready to listen to Belgian pleas to close UNAMIR down. After Somalia, the military was suspicious of all UN peacekeeping operations, and the death of the Belgians seemed to make the dangers even more obvious.

James Woods, Deputy Asst, Secretary of Defense, 1986-94: Under the UN, you get your throat cut. You get mutilated. You can't defend yourself. You're put in harm's way with no way of defending yourself. And this is another reason why you wouldn't want to get identified with a UN operation. It's just a horrible example of a UN operation.

Narrator: In New York, at the American mission to the UN, headed by Ambassador Madeline Albright, the reaction was much the same.

Interviewer: What were your instructions, or what was the attitude of your superiors at the U.S. UN Mission?

Michael Barnett, U.S. Mission to the UN, 1994: The general attitude was that "We now have to close down the operation."

Interviewer: Close it down?

Michael Barnett: Close it down.

Interviewer: Close it down, even though that's what the Hutu extremists, the killers, had wanted you to do?

Michael Barnett: In retrospect, it's clear that that's in fact what they intended to happen. But if peacekeepers are in jeopardy and you don't have the capacity to protect them, then the Security Council must do the responsible thing, which is to withdraw the peacekeepers from harm's way.

Narrator: At the school of Don Bosco, the peacekeepers were still saving lives. A thousand refugees had now taken shelter here. The niece of the murdered politician, Lando, had been sent by her parents, who believed here, surely, there were enough UN soldiers to protect her.

Nausicaa Habimana: *[through interpreter]* We didn't feel in danger at all because we could see that the blue berets were with us. We weren't worried at all. We felt really safe and secure.

Interviewer: They thought they'd be safe with the United Nations.

Capt. Luc Lemaire: Yes, they should be protected by the United Nations groups.

Interviewer: So they came there to find safety?

Capt. Luc Lemaire: Certainly. Yes.

Narrator: FRONTLINE has learned that the UN's men on the ground did signal the plight of Tutsi civilians to the secretariat in New York. As early as the second day of the killings, a secret cable warned that ordinary people were being targeted simply because of their ethnic origin.

Cable: "All UNAMIR camps have sheltered civilians terrified by the ruthless campaign of ethnic cleansing and terror."

Narrator: But in New York, once more a crucial warning went unheeded. Rather than telling the security council the violence was ethnic cleansing, the secretariat described it as a breakdown in the ceasefire, much easier to dismiss as an internal matter for Rwanda.

Interviewer: Surely it wasn't very difficult to realize that this could be the start of an unfolding genocide?

Iqbal Riza, Chief of Staff to UN Secretary General: No, not— well, it may not have been very difficult, and maybe we made a second mistake, but certainly, in the first few days neither the people on the ground, except for that one sentence, or we here, knew that this was a planned genocide.

Philip Gourevitch, Author, *We Wish to Inform You...*: It's extraordinary, at the least, that those who were charged with maintaining the Rwanda mission at the UN can now plead that they didn't recognize what was going on. It was murky, but this was not a top secret program. The signs were on the surface. They were on the radio. They were in the newspapers. You could buy them at any street corner. You could hear them at any rally. You didn't have to go looking.

Narrator: By the 11th of April, four days after the genocide began, the Red Cross was estimating that tens of thousands had already been killed in Rwanda.

At Don Bosco the killers continued to flaunt themselves in front of their prey. By April 11, 2,000 civilians had taken refuge in the school. But with the Belgian campaign to get UNAMIR out of Rwanda close to success, everyone realized the troops might leave, and the refugees now made a remarkable request of Captain Lemaire.

Capt. Luc Lemaire: They were afraid to be murdered by the machetes. When they heard we could leave in the following days they say, "Please don't do that. If you have to leave, please, we ask you to be shot down by your machine gun." They would rather be shot down by our machine gun than be murdered by machetes.

Interviewer: Sooner a United Nations bullet than a machete?

Capt. Luc Lemaire: That's it.

That afternoon the Belgian soldiers left Don Bosco. Their commanders had ordered them to withdraw to the airport. When the refugees realized they were being abandoned, they began to crowd around the last of the departing UN vehicles.

Florida Ngulinzira: *[through interpreter]* All of the refugees were running in front of the trucks in order to stop them leaving. And I remember hanging on to a UNAMIR truck and asking the soldier, "Are you really abandoning us? We'll all be killed. Why are you leaving?"

Lt. Jean-Noel Lecomte, UNAMIR: I was obliged to fire in the air to open the path to the last vehicles because there were all these people around there, all over the vehicle.

Interviewer: So you were firing into the air to clear a path—

Lt. Jean-Noel Lecomte: Yes.

Interviewer: —through the refugees. Was that the first time you'd fired your weapon in Rwanda?

Lt. Jean-Noel Lecomte: Yes, for the first time.

Nausicaa Habimana: *[through interpreter]* After we heard those shots in the air, we were frightened because it was as if it were a signal to show the Interahamwe that they had gone, so that they could come in and kill everyone.

Interviewer: So what can you say to the parents of a young girl who put her under the protection of the United Nations only for you to abandon her?

Capt. Luc Lemaire: I cannot say anything because it was so, and we had no choice.

Narrator: As the Belgian soldiers drove away, the killers moved in. The fate of the refugees would not be known for several days.

In the first days of the genocide, the Clinton administration was focused not on the Tutsis, but on what was happening to the 255 Americans in Rwanda.

Pres. Bill Clinton: It is a very tense situation, and I just want to assure the families of those who are there that we are doing everything we possibly can to be on top of the situation, to take all appropriate steps to try to assure the safety of our citizens there.

Narrator: In the first days of the killing, France, Belgium and Italy all sent troops to Rwanda, but they were under national rather than UN command. They'd been sent not to stop the killing, but to rescue their own citizens, like the white staff at Kigali's psychiatric hospital. But the hospital had become a makeshift refuge where Tutsis were hiding from the killers in the surrounding fields.

Katelijne Hermans, Belgian Television: At a certain moment, they were shouting. We heard people crying. And I still remember

Frank Connor

Don Cheadle, as Paul Rusesabagina, and the refugees at the Mille Collines watch
as they are abandoned by French and Belgian troops.

now. I turned my head, and I saw tens, hundreds of people coming.
They came just to ask for help. And then when they came nearer,
they put themselves on their knees. They put their hands in the air.
They knew there was shooting around. They told us, "There are
military guys here around, and yet they are against us. They are
there to kill us. So please take us away. Take us with you."

One woman started to speak and started to explain why they
were afraid and what was happening to them. And she started
begging us to take her and the others with us. She was speaking to
me, a woman to a woman, saying, "I am afraid there are—those
men, I am afraid that they will rape me."

It was very hard to say, "I cannot help you." I was not talking to
hundreds of people, I was talking to one woman, and that's very
hard to say. But it's like that. I couldn't do anything. But they were
as afraid as the white people over there. And they just said, "We

will be killed. Please take us with you. Bring us to another place, but don't leave us here."

So we left. For the white people it's over, but we knew the hundreds that stayed, and we heard the shooting the moment we left. So it was clear for me that hell starts for them.

Narrator: Back at the airport, French soldiers were escorting their citizens to safety, along with French diplomats and the embassy dog. They did not evacuate the embassy's Tutsi staff who were later murdered. The Americans, too, were airlifted out.

The new Western troops were only on the ground for a few days. UNAMIR commanders say that if their governments had ordered them to stay, the massacres could have been stopped.

Brig. Henry Anyidoho, Deputy Commander, UNAMIR: Had they been deployed, we had enough troops.

Interviewer: So there was a moment? There was a moment when there were troops on the ground?

Brig. Henry Anyidoho: There was a moment. We just missed it. It was a fleeting opportunity, and we just missed it.

Interviewer: Why was it missed?

Brig. Henry Anyidoho: Because there was no political will?

Katelijne Hermans: The only mandate was "Evacuate white people." It could have been another mandate.

Interviewer: Could have been different?

Katelijne Hermans: It could have been different. But somebody has to decide that it will be different, and nobody took the decision.

Narrator: At the psychiatric hospital, the killers had moved in after the Belgian soldiers left. Almost all of these people were murdered.

Belgium mourned its dead soldiers. Confident other countries would soon follow its lead, the government now took the fateful decision to withdraw its troops from Rwanda. The officer who'd first reported the informant's warning of genocide three months earlier was told to lead the retreat.

Col. Luc Marchal: I was ashamed to execute that kind of decision. You don't react as a military, but you react just as a normal human being. And when you know that kind of action will just have a consequence, the losses of thousands and thousands of lives, it's not easy to—to live with that.

Narrator: By April 21, two weeks after the killing began, the Red Cross estimate was that tens, perhaps hundreds of thousands were now dead. In New York, with the scale of the killing becoming public, the UN Security Council arrived to decide the future of its mission in Rwanda. It was an historic chance to fulfill its promise "Never again."

By a bizarre coincidence, one of the rotating delegations whose turn it was to sit on the council and decide UNAMIR's future represented the killers.

Chairman: I now give the floor to the representative of Rwanda.

Narrator: But on this day, everybody was too polite to interrupt the public rituals and call the ambassador from Rwanda to account.

Michael Barnett, U.S. Mission to the UN, 1994: Nobody said, "Stop it." Nobody said, "Your presence here disgusts me." Nobody said, "Why don't you just get out of the room?" There was never a real moment in which they dressed him down because if you did, you would be breaking the rules of the club.

Chairman: I thank the representative of Rwanda.

Narrator: The Security Council voted unanimously to withdraw most of its troops from Rwanda. They decided to leave a token force of just over 200 men, who had no chance of stopping the massacre.

Michael Barnett: People in the Security Council should have been ashamed. There should have been remorse. There should have been contrition. There should have been some degree of, you know, internal contestation. But there was none of that. And I began to sort of really wonder what was it about myself, what was it about the process that could allow lots of really smart, good, responsible people to come to such decisions.

Narrator: Two days after the Security Council's vote came the news of what had happened to the Tutsis the UN troops had already abandoned at Don Bosco.

The tiny force left behind in Rwanda spent much of its time pinned down by the crossfire between the Hutus and the encroaching Tutsi rebels. The Tutsis had invaded after the genocide began.

Nausicaa Habimana: *[through interpreter]* I heard on the radio that UNAMIR had left Rwanda, and for me they were utter swines because they began by giving us shelter, and then they left us in the hands of killers who did us much harm and who killed our families.

Narrator: Now that it was clear the world was giving the killers a free hand, they went to work across the whole country, from big towns to tiny hilltop villages. In Nyarubuye, several hundred Tutsis had fled to the Catholic church. But in Rwanda there were no more sanctuaries.

Valentina Iribagiza: *[through interpreter]* We were pretending to be dead. They took stones and smashed the heads of the bodies. They took little children and smashed their heads together. When they found someone breathing, they pulled them out and finished them off. They killed my family. I saw them kill my papa and my brother, but I didn't see what happened to my mother.

Karel Kovanda, Czech Ambassador to UN, 1994: When you come from Central Europe, one has a sense of what holocausts are about. You recognize one when you see one.

Interviewer: In your case because?

Karel Kovanda: A lot of my father's family perished in the Holocaust.

Interviewer: And did you feel here it was happening again, or is that—

Karel Kovanda: Oh, yes. Very definitely. Yes, here it was happening again.

Narrator: But when the Security Council met privately to discuss Rwanda in this small consultation room, it was made clear that calling the killing genocide was just not in the interests of the UN

Michael Barnett: By mid to late April, people in the Security Council knew it was genocide, but refused to call it as such because, ultimately, one understood that if you used the term "genocide," then you might be forced to act. And when someone suggested that maybe they should call a genocide a genocide, they were quietly reminded that perhaps they should not use such language.

Karel Kovanda: I know that I personally had an important conversation with one of my superiors in Prague who at American behest suggested that they lay off.

Interviewer: Lay off calling it genocide?

Karel Kovanda: Yeah. Lay off pushing Rwanda, in general, and calling it genocide specifically.

Interviewer: So the Americans had actually talked to your government back in Prague and said, "Don't let's call it genocide."

Karel Kovanda: In Prague or in Washington, but they were talking to my superiors, yes.

Narrator: In fact, FRONTLINE has learned that a secret intelligence report by the State Department had called the killings genocide as early as the end of April. But publicly the government was still hedging and finding it difficult to defend its position that the slaughter was not a genocide.

Reporter: *[April 28, 1994]* Does the State Department have a view as to whether or not what is happening could be genocide?

Christine Shelly, State Department Spokeswoman: Well, as I think you know, the use of the term "genocide" has a very precise legal meaning, although it's not strictly a legal determination. There are other factors in there, as well. When—in looking at a situation to make a determination about that, before we begin to use that term, we have to know as much as possible about the facts of the situation and—

Alan Elsner, Reuters: The answers they were giving were really non-answers. They would talk in incredibly bureaucratic language. In a sense, it was almost like a caricature. If you look at it now, it looks utterly ridiculous. These were all kind of artful ways of doing nothing, which is what they were determined to do.

Christine Shelly: This is a more complicated issue to address, and we're certainly looking into this extremely carefully right now. But I'm not able to look at all of those criteria at this moment and—

Narrator: By May the White House was organizing confidential daily conferences on Rwanda with officials across Washington by secure video link. In this secret world, one reason for not calling the killing genocide became disturbingly clear.

Tony Marley, State Department Military Adviser, 1992-95: One official even asked a question as to what possible outcome there might be on the congressional elections later that year were the administration to acknowledge that this was genocide taking place in Rwanda and be seen to do nothing about it. The concern obviously was whether it would result in a loss of votes for the party in the November elections.

Interviewer: What was your reaction?

Tony Marley: I was stunned because I didn't see what bearing that had on whether or not genocide was, in fact, taking place in Rwanda. Partisan political vote-gathering in the U.S. had no bearing on the objective reality in Rwanda.

Narrator: The objective reality of what was happening in Rwanda couldn't be kept quiet forever. Rwanda's dead had begun to float downstream into the outside world. The country was literally overflowing with corpses.

In his inter-agency meetings, Tony Marley argued, "Let's at least send a few thousand dollars worth of rubber rafts and boat hooks to fish the bodies out of the water."

Tony Marley: If we weren't going to stop the killing inside Rwanda, we could at least minimize the disease risk to those citizens of the neighboring countries that were now endangered potentially by disease, that had no involvement in the Rwandan conflict one way or the other.

Interviewer: How did the military react to your idea?

Tony Marley: It was not acted upon. Again, there was great reluctance on the part of many defense officials to have any U.S. involvement.

Radio Broadcast: *[subtitles]* All Tutsis will perish. They will disappear from the earth.

Narrator: Marley also proposed the Pentagon begin jamming the Rwandan state radio that was promoting the killing.

Interviewer: How did that go down?

Tony Marley: It was not favorably reacted upon. In fact, one lawyer from the Pentagon made the argument that that would be contrary to the US constitutional protection of freedom of the press, freedom of speech.

Interviewer: So the lawyers were saying that closing down the hate radio would have been censorship?

Tony Marley: Correct. As I understand their position, yes.

Narrator: By mid-May, an estimated 500,000 had been murdered in Rwanda now numbered 500,000. It seemed there would be no end to the killing, nor to the endless Security Council debates in New York.

Interviewer: Did you feel that lives were at stake in that room?

Karel Kovanda, Czech UN Ambassador, 1994: Oh, heaven— heaven knows, yes. Yes. There were lives at stake, lives which were just like sand disappearing through our hands day after day. You've got 10,000 today, 12,000 tomorrow, and if you don't do something today, then tomorrow there will be more. If you don't do something this week, then next week there will be more with, no end in sight at the time. No end in sight.

Narrator: But it still wasn't too late. Hundreds of thousands of Tutsis had somehow survived. Eight thousand had taken refuge at the Catholic seminary of Kabgui. But such havens were becoming little more than concentration camps. The victims made desperate pleas to an indifferent world.

Refugee: *["BBC Newsnight," May 16, 1994] [through interpreter]* They're attacking us. It's unbelievable. They come in here and take the old and the young out of the camp and kill them using knives and machetes. It defies imagination, and there's nothing we can do.

Narrator: Then suddenly, the UN seemed to have a change of heart.

United States UN Official: *[Security Council meeting, May 17, 1994]* Mr. President, the cries of the victims in Rwanda have been heard calling upon the Security Council to act. The sheer magnitude of the humanitarian disaster in that tragic country demands action.

Narrator: Now saying it was deeply affected by the tragedy, the Security Council voted to increase its force in Rwanda to over 5,000 men with a clear mandate to protect civilians.

Sir David Hannay, British Ambassador to UN: The priority now must be to ensure the early deployment of the troops needed for these tasks.

Narrator: But the Security Council did not set a timetable for deploying the new troops, and some insiders believed it was all a sham.

Interviewer: When the Security Council voted for a stronger UN-AMIR, what did you think was actually going to happen?

Michael Barnett, U.S. Mission to the UN, 1994: Nothing was going to happen. Nothing was. And that's what happened.

Interviewer: Nothing.

Michael Barnett: Nothing.

Interviewer: Because?

Michael Barnett: Because this was a document that looked great on paper, but didn't have really much of a chance of ever being implemented.

Interviewer: Because?

Michael Barnett: Because fundamentally, member states weren't going to provide the resources to carry out that plan.

Narrator: If a new UNAMIR mission were to save lives, it would need more armored personnel carriers, or APCs. The UN had only five in Rwanda, not nearly enough to get troops around the country safely. The White House promised to lease UNAMIR 50 more, but the U.S. military, which had the job of delivering them, was still afraid of being dragged into a conflict it could not control and seemed to seize any opportunity for delay.

James Woods, Deputy Asst, Secretary of Defense, 1986-94: It became almost a joke as to the length of time and the, you know, ever-emerging details of things that had to be decided in order to get the bloody APCs on their way. And they got all bogged down into issues of the exact terms of a lease, what color, who would paint them where, what color, what kind of stenciling would go on and all of the other little details.

Interviewer: I mean were people aware that while this was going on, people were dying?

James Woods: Oh, sure. Of course.

Interviewer: And?

James Woods: And—well, where were the Belgians? I don't see the British Gurkha battalions, either. Where was everybody? Everybody was hiding.

Narrator: The Americans finally delivered the APCs, but only to neighboring Uganda, where they stayed until the killing was over. Meanwhile, the Clinton administration was still playing word games.

Christine Shelly, State Department Spokeswoman: *[June 10, 1994]* We have every reason to believe that acts of genocide have occurred.

Reporter: How many acts of genocide does it take to make genocide?

Christine Shelly: That's just not a question that I'm in a position to answer.

Reporter: Is it true that you have specific guidance not to use the word "genocide" in isolation, but always preface it with these words "acts of"?

Christine Shelly: I have guidance which—which—to which I—which I try to use as best as I can. I'm not—I have—there are formulations that we are using that we are trying to be consistent in our use of. I don't have an absolute categorical prescription against something, but I have the definitions. I have a phraseology which has been carefully examined and arrived at to—

Narrator: In mid-July, the Tutsi-led guerrillas finally won the war. The killers were defeated. The Hutu genocide was over. With their hoes and machetes, the extremists had killed three times faster than the Nazis. An estimated 800,000 people had been murdered in 100 days.

Four years later, President Clinton made his pilgrimage of contrition to Rwanda.

Pres. Bill Clinton: I have come today to pay the respects of my nation to all who suffered and all who perished in the Rwandan genocide. We did not act quickly enough after the killing began. We should not have allowed—

Narrator: In his speech, the president would use the word "genocide" 11 times.

Pres. Bill Clinton: We did not immediately call these crimes by their rightful name, genocide.

Michael Barnett: It was meaningless. It was hollow. It was unclear to me what he was apologizing for and for whom he was apologizing. He didn't say "I take personal responsibility for the failure of the United States, the international community to do something to stop genocide." He made, as I recall, some kind of vague reference to the failure of the international community to act and to help the Rwandans in their hour of need.

Pres. Bill Clinton: It may seem strange to you here, especially the many of you who lost members of your family, but all over the world there were people like me sitting in offices day after day after day who did not fully appreciate the depth and the speed with which you were being engulfed by this unimaginable terror.

James Woods, Deputy Asst, Secretary of Defense, 1986-94: Well, I would say that responsibility starts at the top. And I know the president went to Rwanda and apologized and said he didn't really understand because he wasn't properly informed. This is not true. They were informed. They were adequately informed.

Narrator: Before his speech to government officials, President Clinton had a private audience with a few survivors of the genocide and listened silently to their horrifying stories. Afterward he presented the president of Rwanda with a plaque honoring the victims of genocide. President Clinton would spend just three and a half hours in Kigali. He never left the airport, and the engines of Air Force One never shut down.

Philip Gourevitch, *The New Yorker*: We talk about Rwanda as a failure of US policy—a failure to intervene, a failure to recognize what was going on, and a failure to take action to stop genocide. But if you look at the Clinton administration's approach to it throughout the entire period, what you really see is that it was actually a success of a policy not to intervene. It wasn't a failure to act. The decision was not to act. And at that we succeeded greatly.

I think that anybody who still believes that the world will not let it happen again, who believes the words "Never again," is deluding themselves dangerously.

III.
History

President Paul Kagame speaks at the tenth anniversary commemoration of the 1994 genocide. A banner reads "Never again," in French.

A Brief History of Rwanda

Rwanda has a long, complex history, but like many African countries, its history is mostly unrecorded. Rwanda did not even exist as a firm entity prior to the late 1800s; until then, the area was a loose conglomeration of two main ethnic groups: Hutu and the Tutsi.

The Tutsi people were wealthy land and livestock owners who arrived in the area now known as Rwanda in the fourteenth or fifteenth century. The Hutu people already inhabited the area and actually outnumbered the Tutsis, but the Tutsi minority was gradually able to subjugate the Hutus, eventually ruling them in a system of feudal monarchy. This ethnic division existed with few tensions for several hundred years.

In 1894 the first Westerners arrived in Rwanda, and by 1899, without resistance from the native inhabitants, the Germans turned Rwanda into a protectorate as part of German East Africa. During World War I, the Belgian Army, based in neighboring Zaire (the present day Democratic Republic of the Congo), took control of Rwanda. The Belgian takeover was solidified after the war by the League of Nations with a joint territorial mandate for "Ruanda-Urundi" encompassing present-day Rwanda and Burundi.

In governing its new territory, the Belgian authorities used the existing Tutsi monarchy to their advantage in controlling the population, but in doing so they exacerbated the institutionalized differences between the ethnic groups. Belgian rule and extreme preference for the Tutsis—often relegating Hutus to the

Courtesy of the National Museum of African Art, Smithsonian Institute

King Musinga and the royal family, Rwanda, c. 1910.

fringes of society—created huge tensions in the country, which flared up post–World War II. In the 1950s, the Belgians began reforms to correct the problems and establish a democratic government, but the Tutsi traditionalists resisted. The Belgians then turned on their previous allies, encouraging a Hutu rebellion in 1959 that threw the Tutsis out of power. An election was held, leading the way for Hutu majority rule and independence from Belgium in 1962.

Post-independence, inefficiency and corruption ran rampant in the country, and Major General Juvenal Habyarimana, a Hutu, staged a military coup in 1973, taking over the country as dictator and banning all political activity except for that of his own party. Habyarimana ruled the country with an iron fist until finally bending to pressure from the United Nations to reform Rwanda

Readers look at a newspaper carrying the photograph of Rwandan Felicien Kabuga wanted by the United States on June 12, 2002, in Nairobi. The United States stepped up a search for the alleged masterminds of Rwanda's 1994 genocide by publishing a "wanted" photograph in Kenyan newspapers of the wealthy Rwandan accused of helping finance the killings.

in 1990. At the same time, a group mostly made up of Tutsi Rwandan exiles formed the Rwandan Patriotic Front (RPF) and invaded Rwanda from Uganda, beginning a civil war. Peace talks were solidified in the Arusha Accords in 1994, which promised democratic reforms.

On the way back from signing the Accords, on April 6, 1994, Major General Habyarimana and the President of Burundi were assassinated in a plane crash by members of their own parties, who subsequently blamed the Tutsis for the deaths. That very night, a pre-planned execution of high-ranking Tutsi officials and Hutu moderates began. Over the next three days, virtually any ranking Tutsi or moderate Hutu in power was systematically executed, and the violence didn't stop there. Roaming bands of an organized Hutu militia known as the Interahamwe roamed the country, and the killing spread exponentially to all corners of

Courtesy of UNHCR

During the genocide, more than three million refugees left Rwanda.

Rwanda for the next three months with nothing to stop it. Even as the Red Cross estimated that hundreds of thousands were being murdered, mostly by machete, the United Nations reduced its peacekeeping force from 2,500 to 270 soldiers. The RPF ultimately invaded again from Uganda, prevailing and bringing an end to the genocide in July 1994. Most Hutu extremists fled to Zaire.

Over the course of the genocide nearly one million people were killed, and more than three million fled to other countries, creating the world's worst ever refugee crisis. Only then did the West respond, launching the largest aid effort in human history, which finally concluded two years later in March of 1996. Soon after, war broke out in several neighboring countries causing almost all of the refugees to return home by 1997.

Post-genocide, a Unity government was formed, and in 2000,

Rwandan President Paul Kagame, left, and Ugandan President Yoweri Museveni, right, hold roses on April 7, 2004, before laying them on the graves at the Memorial Genocide site of Gisozi, during the tenth anniversary commemoration of the 1994 genocide.

Paul Kagame, former head of the RPF, was elected transition president. Kagame was then elected to a regular term in the country's first standard elections in 2003. The United Nations established the International Criminal Tribunal for Rwanda, which has been trying high-level Hutu officials for crimes against humanity, while local governments have resorted to tribal councils, called *gacaca*, to sanction the estimated 80,000 people involved in the genocide.

By 2003, reforms and educational programs were in place that removed any reference to ethnicity in Rwanda; the terms Hutu and Tutsi are now banned from usage, as is any "divisive behavior." Also, the government-funded Rwandan Survivors' Fund receives 5 percent of the country's income, funding countless widows' and orphans' funds. While the country is growing fast, it is still recovering. Population levels are still below 1994 numbers and the nation faces continued problems, including corruption, conflict with neighboring nations (including a long war with the Democratic Republic of the Congo), and one of the worst poverty rates in sub-Sarahan Africa.

Basic Facts: Rwanda

GEOGRAPHY

Rwanda is slightly smaller than the state of Maryland, bordered by Tanzania to the east, Burundi to the south, the Democratic Republic of the Congo to the west, and Uganda to the north.

There are two rainy seasons: February to April and November to January.

Rwanda's main natural resources are gold, cassiterite (tin ore), wolframite (tungsten ore), methane, hydropower, and arable land.

The country is landlocked and mostly made up of savanna grass-land.

PEOPLE

As of July 2004, the population of Rwanda is 7,954,013. It is the most densely populated country in Africa.

The average life expectancy was 39.18 years in 2004.

As of 2003, it's estimated that 51 percent of Rwandans have HIV/AIDS; 250,000 people are living with AIDS.

Eighty-four percent of the population is considered Hutu, 15 percent Tutsi, and the remaining 1 percent Twa/Pygmoid.

The main religions of Rwanda are: Roman Catholic (56 percent), Protestant (26 percent), Adventist (11.1 percent), Muslim (4.6 percent), Indigenous beliefs (.1 percent), or none (1.7 percent).

Approximately 70 percent of the population is literate.

GOVERNMENT

The government is considered a republic, presidential, multi-party system. The legal system is based on German and Belgian civil law systems and customary law.

ECONOMY

Sixty percent of the population is considered below the poverty line.

There is a labor force of 4.6 million, with 90 percent of the workers in agriculture.

The most common export commodities are coffee, tea, hides, and tin ore.

All facts adapted from *The World Factbook 2004*. For more information go to www.cia.gov/cia/publications/factbook/geos/rw.html.

Timeline: The Rwandan Crisis

1918	Rwanda-Burundi is made a League of Nations protectorate governed by Belgium. The minority Tutsi ethnic group is favored over the majority Hutu and given privileges like Western-style education.
1926	The Belgians introduce a system of ethnic identity cards differentiating Hutus from Tutsis.
1961-62	The Belgians withdraw and Rwanda and Burundi become separate, independent countries. A Hutu revolution in Rwanda causes thousands of Tutsis to flee.
1963	The further massacre of Rwandan Tutsis occurs in response to attacks by exiled Tutsis in Burundi. More refugees leave, and it is estimated that half of the Tutsi population is living outside Rwanda.
1973	The Tutsis are forced out of universities, and a fresh outbreak of killings begins. The army chief of staff seizes power, and Tutsis are restricted to 9 percent of all available jobs.

Oct. 1990

Guerillas from the Rwandan Patriotic Front invade Rwanda from Uganda; the RPF is mostly made up of Tutsis. A ceasefire is signed on March 29, 1991.

Dec. 1990

The Hutu paper *Kangura* ("Wake Up!") publishes the inflammatory "Ten Commandments of the Hutus."

1990-91

Thousands of Tutsis are killed in separate massacres around the country, and the Rwandan army forms and trains the Hutu-dominated Interahamwe militia ("those who stand together").

1992

The Hutu militia has stockpiled more than half a million machetes.

Nov. 1992

Dr. Leon Mugusera, a Hutu extremist and senior member of Rwandan President Habyarimana's party, appeals to the Hutus to "wipe [the Tutsis] all out."

Jan. 1993

The CIA issues a report anticipating extensive ethnic violence in Rwanda.

Feb. 1993

The RPF again invades Rwanda. Hutu extremists cite the invasion as proof the Tutsis aim to eliminate them, and begin calling for preemptive measures.

March 1993

An international commission finds more than 2,000 Tutsis have been killed since 1990.

Blid Alsbirk

Hundreds of machetes fall out of a broken wooden crate during Paul Rusesabagina's (Don Cheadle) visit to George Rutaganda (Hakeem Kae-Kazim), depicting the Hutu militia's stockpiling of weapons.

Aug. 1993   President Habyarimana (a Hutu) and the RPF
                 sign a peace accord. A month later, the presi-
                 dent has still not implemented the regulations
                 of the accord.

Oct. 1993   Eighteen elite U.S. soldiers are killed in So-
                 malia. The incident receives wide attention.
                 The United Nations Assistance Mission for
                 Rwanda (UNAMIR) is created, with Canadian
                 Brigadier- General Roméo Dallaire as its force
                 commander. Of the 2,500 UN troops eventu-
                 ally deployed under his command, there are
                 no U.S. soldiers.

Dec. 1993   The CIA learns the Rwandan government has
                 imported roughly 4 million tons of small arms
                 through Belgium. Dallaire receives a letter from
                 well-connected Hutu military officers claiming
                 the militias are preparing exterminations.
                 Rumors of "death lists" are widely spread. The
                 RTLMC radio station has begun accusing the
                 UN peacekeepers of being in league with
                 the Tutsis.

Jan. 1994   A reliable Hutu informant offers to lead Dal-
                 laire to large stockpiles of weapons. Dallaire
                 informs the UN of his intention to raid the
                 stockpiles. He receives a fax from the office of
                 Kofi Annan, then in charge of the Department
                 of Peacekeeping Operations, forbidding the ac-
                 tion. Despite Dallaire's subsequent pleas, the
                 order stands.

Rwandan refugees flee into neighboring countries.

Courtesy of UNHCR

April 6, 1994   President Habyarimana and the president of
                     Burundi, Cyprien Ntaryamira, are killed in a
                     plane crash orchestrated by Hutu extremists to
                     stop the implementation of the peace accords.
                     The organized murder of all high-profile Tutsis
                     and moderate Hutus begins that night.

April 7, 1994   Thousands of Tutsis are already dead but the
                     UN peacekeeping troops (UNAMIR) "stand
                     by" so as not to overstep their "monitoring"
                     mandate. Ten Belgian UN peacekeepers, who
                     had been dispatched to the home of Prime
                     Minister Agathe Uwilingiyimana, are mutilated
                     and killed, along with the prime minister.

April 9, 1994   Foreign governments send troops to evacuate
                     their citizens from Rwanda. No Rwandans are
                     rescued.

April 10, 1994   Dallaire appeals for additional troops and a
                     stronger mandate. Discussing the U.S. evacua-
                     tion on *Face the Nation*, Senate minority leader
                     Bob Dole says, "The Americans are out, and as
                     far as I'm concerned, in Rwanda, that ought to
                     be the end of it."

April 11, 1994   The Red Cross estimates that tens of thousands
                     of Rwandans have already been murdered dur-
                     ing the first few days of the conflict.

April 21, 1994   The UN Security Council votes unanimously
                     to withdraw most of the UNAMIR troops.

April 28, 1994   State Department spokeswoman Christine
                     Shelly renounces the term "genocide" when
                     asked about the attacks.

A camp for Rwandan refugees.

April 30, 1994   Tens of thousands of refugees flee Rwanda into Tanzania, Burundi, and Zaire.

May 3, 1994   President Bill Clinton signs a Presidential Decision Directive that limits U.S. military involvement in international peacekeeping operations.

May 11, 1994   State Department spokesman Michael McCurry says the department has not made any legal determination as to whether the events in Rwanda are considered genocide.

May 13, 1994   The UN Security Council prepares to vote on restoring UNAMIR's strength in Rwanda; the vote is delayed for four days by American UN Ambassador Madeleine Albright.

© David Turnley/Corbis

In 1994, thousands of abandoned machetes collected at the border of Rwanda and Tanzania: Hutu refugees fleeing Rwanda were allowed across the border on the condition that they leave behind their weapons.

May 17, 1994	A UN Security Council resolution commits to sending 5,500 troops and admits "acts of genocide may have been committed."
mid-May 1994	The International Red Cross estimates 500,000 Rwandans have been killed.
June 22, 1994	UN forces still have not been sent to Rwanda, so the Security Council authorizes the deployment of French forces to create a "safe area." Regardless, the killing of Tutsis continues.
July 14, 1994	Roughly 6,000 people per hour enter the French safe area.
mid-July 1994	The Tutsi RPF forces capture Kigali and the genocide is over. Over a period of 100 days, almost one million Rwandans were murdered.

Resources

Books

Berkeley, Bill, *The Graves Are Not Yet Full: Race, Tribe, and Power in the Heart of Africa*, Basic Books, 2001.

Dallaire, Roméo, *Shake Hands with the Devil: The Failure of Humanity in Rwanda*, Carroll & Graf, 2004.

Des Forges, Alison, *Leave None to Tell the Story: Genocide in Rwanda*, Human Rights Watch, 1999.

Destexhe, Alain, Alison Marschner (Translator), William Shawcross (Foreword), *Rwanda and Genocide in the Twentieth Century*, New York University Press, 1995.

Gourevitch, Philip, *We Wish To Inform You That Tomorrow We Will Be Killed With Our Families: Stories from Rwanda*, Farrar Straus Giroux, 1998.

Keane, Fergal, *Season of Blood: A Rwandan Journey*, Viking Books, 1995.

Melvern, Linda, *A People Betrayed: The Role of the West in Rwanda's Genocide*, Zed Books, 2000.
　　—*Conspiracy to Murder: The Rwanda Genocide*, Verso Books, 2004.

Off, Carol, *The Lion, the Fox and the Eagle: A Story of Generals and Justice in Rwanda and Yugoslavia*, Random House Canada, 2000.

Peterson, Scott, *Me Against My Brother: At War in Somalia, Sudan, and Rwanda*, Routledge, 2000.

Power, Samantha, *A Problem From Hell: America and the Age of Genocide*, Basic Books, 2002.

Prunier, Gérard, *The Rwanda Crisis: History of a Genocide*, Columbia University Press, 1995.

Rwanda: Death, Despair, and Defiance, African Rights, 1995.

Salem, Richard A. (Editor), Hillary Rodham Clinton (Foreword), *Witness to Genocide: The Children of Rwanda: Drawings by Child Survivors of the Rwandan Genocide of 1994*, Friendship Press, 2000.

Web Resources

The Latest News from Rwanda
allafrica.com/rwanda

International Criminal Tribunal for Rwanda
www.ictr.org

U.S. Department of State Profile of Rwanda
www.state.gov/r/pa/ei/bgn/2861.htm

The Rwanda Information Exchange
www.rwanda.net

UN Foundation
www.unfoundation.org

The National Security Archive
www.gwu.edu/~nsarchiv/NSAEBB/NSAEBB53/index.html

The official movie site
www.hotelrwanda.com

Feature Films

100 Days, written and directed by Nick Hughes (Vivid Features, 2001)

Documentaries

Gacaca, Living Together Again In Rwanda?, directed by Anne Aghion (First Run / Icarus Films, 2002)

Ghosts of Rwanda, written and directed by Greg Barker (Frontline, 2004)
www.pbs.org/wgbh/pages/frontline/shows/ghosts/

Shake Hands With The Devil, directed by Peter Raymont (White Pine Pictures, 2004)

The Triumph of Evil, written by Steve Bradshaw & Ben Loeterman (Frontline, 1999)
www.pbs.org/wgbh/pages/frontline/shows/evil/

Organizations Working in Rwanda

International Fund for Rwanda
www.internationalfundforrwanda.org

Business Council for Peace
www.bpeace.com

The Office of the United Nations High Commissioner for
Refugees in Rwanda
www.unhcr.ch/cgi-bin/texis/vtx/country?iso=rwa

Rwanda: Advanced Healing and Reconciliation developed by the
Trauma Research Education and Training Institute and UMASS-
Amherst
www.heal-reconcile-rwanda.org/

Remembering Rwanda: The Rwanda 10th Anniversary Memorial
Project
www.visiontv.ca/RememberRwanda/main_pf.htm

Through the Eyes of Children: The Rwanda Project
www.rwandaproject.org

Rwandan Genocide Survivors Organizations

AVEGA-AGAHOZO: Association of Genocide Widows
www.avega.org.rw

IV.
The Screenplay

"Now that the film is finished, I am satisfied. I cannot tell you that I'll forget, but I forgive—and my voice at long last can be heard. What happened in Rwanda can be told to many people, maybe more people than we even imagine will listen. The story might serve as a wake-up call to the international community—the genocide was watched and not stopped until it was already over. Then people can see what is happening in the Congo, and in Burundi, and in many other parts of the world which are never on the radios, on the televisions, places nobody talks about. At long last, the message has been told. This is my satisfaction."

—Paul Rusesabagina, 2004

HOTEL RWANDA

by

Keir Pearson & Terry George

Final Draft

BLACK SCREEN.

>   RADIO ANNOUNCER (V.O.)
>   When people ask me, good listeners,
>   "Why do I hate the Tutsi?" I say
>   "Read our history." The Tutsi were
>   collaborators for the Belgian
>   colonists. They stole our Hutu
>   land, they whipped us. Now they
>   have come back, these Tutsi rebels.
>   They are cockroaches. They are
>   murderers. Rwanda is our Hutu
>   land. We are the majority. They
>   are a minority of traitors and
>   invaders. We will squash the
>   infestation. We will wipe out the
>   RPF rebels. This is RTLM, Hutu
>   power radio. Stay alert -- watch
>   your neighbors.

CAPTION: FADE IN

          Kigali, 1994

CAPTION: FADE OUT

EXT. KIGALI AIRPORT - DAY

A run-down (sixties) airport, peeling in the heat.

A mad traffic jam of cars, vans, motorbikes all stopped at a checkpoint where a RWANDAN POLICEMAN blows his whistle, waves some on and stops others as bored Rwandan soldiers look on.

CLOSE ON: A white van pulls out of traffic, a balls-out case of line jumping. HORNS, OBSCENITIES.

A HAND: Extends from the passenger side of the van, Rwandan francs pressed neatly between the thumb and palm.

In the passenger seat PAUL RUSESABAGINA, late 30's, flashes a smile. He is dressed in a sharp blue suit (always dressed in a neat suit and tie, it is a matter of pride).

A quick shake of hands. Money passes from one to the other.

>   PAUL
>   Good to see you, sir.

>   POLICEMAN
>   Thank you.

Paul nods to driver and they continue on.

SIGN READS: WELCOME TO KIGALI AIRPORT

EXT. KIGALI AIRPORT - RUNWAY - DAY

DUBE looks on as an attendant removes a large polystyrene box
from a Sabena jet. Dube places money in the attendant's
pocket.

                    ATTENDANT
          Thank you.

                    DUBE
          Thank you.

Paul talks to some airline pilots.

                    PILOT
          These are for you, sir. They're
          fresh from Havana.

Pilot hands a box of Cuban cigars to Paul.

                    PAUL
          Oh wonderful. Next time you are
          there, tell Fidel that I said
          hello.

Paul shakes the pilot's hand.

                    PAUL
          Good to see you, gentlemen.

EXT. KIGALI STREETS - DAY

The white van, marked "THE HOTEL MILLE COLLINES," whips its
way through Kigali's packed streets and open-air markets.

Paul removes a cigar from the box and smells it.

                    DUBE
          Oh that is a fine cigar, sir.

                    PAUL
          This is a Cohiba cigar. Each one
          is worth ten thousand francs.

Dube reacts, glances at Paul.

                    DUBE
          Ten thousand francs?

                        PAUL
          Yes, yes. But it is worth more to
          me than ten thousand francs.

                        DUBE
          What do you mean, sir?

                        PAUL
          If I give a businessman ten
          thousand francs, what does that
          matter to him? He's rich. But if
          I give him a Cohiba cigar straight
          from Havana, Cuba. Hey. Now that
          is style, Dube.

Dube nods.

                        DUBE
          Style.

INT. GEORGE RUTAGUNDA'S WAREHOUSE - OFFICE - DAY

CLOSE ON: The flame from a gold lighter lights a Cohiba
cigar.

                        GEORGE
          Cohiba - a fantastic cigar.

Reveal, GEORGE RUTAGUNDA, gold chains, Rolex watch (like an
African mafia boss). Behind him, through the office window,
the Mille Collines van is being loaded with cases of beer.

                        PAUL
          It's the best, eh?

                        GEORGE
          So...you're going to join us at the
          rally today?

                        PAUL
          I will try my best, George, but
          these days I have no time for
          rallies and politics.

Paul shrugs.

                        GEORGE
          Politics is power, Paul. Hutu
          power -- and money.

George turns and picks up an Interahamwe militia shirt. He
tosses it to Paul.

                    GEORGE
          It's time for you to join your
          people.

                    PAUL
          Thank you, George. But time is
          also money. I need six extra cases
          of beer today, along with the
          regular order.

He takes a wad of banknotes from his inside jacket pocket and
places them on the desk. George picks up the stack.

                    GEORGE
          Business is good at the hotel?

                    PAUL
          Oh, it is very good.

                    GEORGE
          I'm always glad to see you, Paul.

INT. GEORGE RUTAGANDA'S WAREHOUSE - OFFICE - DAY

George leads Paul out into the warehouse. As a forklift
lifts a WOODEN CRATE, George angers.

                    GEORGE (TO FORKLIFT DRIVER)
          Hey, hey, put that back! That's
          not beer.

The driver of the forklift, anxiously, spins the machine to
return the crate but it slides off and CRASHES onto the
floor: MACHETES, hundreds of them, spill out. George yells
at a WAREHOUSE WORKER.

                    GEORGE
          You, clear this up.

                    WAREHOUSE WORKER
          Yes, sir.

George glances at Paul, gestures.

                    GEORGE
          Hey, um, Paul, don't worry about
          the Carlsberg, eh? I'll give you
          Heineken and I won't charge you
          extra.

                    PAUL
          Thank you.

George crouches and picks up a machete. He looks at Paul.

>   GEORGE
>   A bargain buy from China. Ten
>   cents each. You know I'll get at
>   least fifty.

>   PAUL
>   At least.

Dube studies the machetes on the ground.

EXT. KIGALI STREETS - DAY

The van speeds through traffic.

>   DUBE
>   George Rutagunda is a bad man.
>   I've heard him on the radio telling
>   the Hutus to kill all the Tutsis.

>   PAUL
>   Rutagunda and his people, they are
>   all fools, Dube. Their time is
>   soon over.

He looks at Dube.

>   PAUL (CONT'D)
>   Anyway, this is business.

More traffic jams. Then at the intersection they see THE
INTERAHAMWE PARADE - a mass of men and women, most in the
same colorful uniform. Line after line, waves all performing
the Interahamwe war dance, in wild hypnotic sync. Many wave
sticks, spears, wooden imitation guns. A large banner reads,
"Hutu Power."

>   DUBE
>   Oh no, it's the Interahamwe.

>   PAUL
>   Do as they say. Pull over.

Dube sinks down behind the wheel.

>   PAUL
>   No, no, no, no, sit up, Dube. Sit
>   up. Smile, Dube. Don't attract
>   attention to yourself.

Dube sits back. Marchers continue to stream down the street,
all around the van.

> DUBE
> Some of these men are my neighbors.
> They know that I am Tutsi.

> GEORGE
> Just smile as if they are friends,
> Dube.

Dube smiles. Marchers continue to pass. One MARCHER stops
and points at Dube.

> MARCHER
> I know this man. He's a Tutsi!

> 2ND MARCHER
> Are you a Tutsi?

Marchers start to gather at the van's window. Dube is
frozen.

Paul lifts up the colorful t-shirt George Rutaganda gave him.

> PAUL
> No, no, no, hey, hey. Hutu power.
> Hutu power, Hutu power.

The marchers back off and the parade passes.

> PAUL (CONT'D)
> Get out of here.

EXT. HOTEL MILLE COLLINES - GROUNDS - DAY

The van turns off the street into the Mille Collines Hotel.
The van doesn't even have to slow as it passes. A sign on
the guard house reads, "WELCOME TO THE HOTEL MILLE COLLINES."

Lush tropical gardens. Peacocks wander the well-manicured
lawns -- an exotic paradise. The van heads to a magnificent
colonial building.

> DUBE
> There's water coming from the box!

> PAUL
> Park here. We'll go in the front.

INT. HOTEL MILLE COLLINES - LOBBY - DAY

Dube is clutching the polystyrene box as Paul leads him and the valet into a magnificent lobby, a tasteful blend of Africa and Europe. Guests stare as water sloshes and spills from the crate.

GREGOIRE, (Hutu) desk clerk, early 30's, throws a look of disapproval. Paul snaps his fingers toward him.

                    PAUL
          Gregoire! Take care of this.

Gregoire ignores Paul.

                    PAUL (CONT'D)
          Gregoire! See to this right away.

JEAN JACQUES, 40's, the Belgian hotel manager, appears. He sees Paul and Dube and the water hitting the floor.

                    JEAN JACQUES
          Dube, this is the lobby. Paul,
          what's going on?

                    PAUL
          I am sorry, sir. It is an
          emergency.

Paul moves on. Jean Jacques is left standing in disbelief.

INT. HOTEL MILLE COLLINES - KITCHEN - DAY

A bustling kitchen. A crowd of cooks gather around as Dube empties the contents into the sink -- live lobsters.

The HEAD CHEF sorts the living lobsters from the dead.

                    HEAD CHEF
          Ten alive, twelve are dead.

                    PAUL
          All right.

Paul thinks for a moment.

                    PAUL (CONT'D)
          Save the shells. Fill them with a
          stuffing. The good meat and
          something local.

                         HEAD CHEF
            Cassava?

                         PAUL
            And, a fish.

                         HEAD CHEF
            And tipali?

                         PAUL
            Yes. We'll call it "fresh lobster
            in a cassava and tipali crust."

Paul fixes his tie. Another crisis solved.

                         DUBE
            Style, sir?

                         PAUL
            Yes, sir.

EXT. HOTEL MILLE COLLINES - GARDEN/SWIMMING POOL - DAY

GENERAL BIZIMUNGU, head of the Hutu-controlled Rwandan army,
sits across from the Canadian COLONEL OLIVER, a senior UN
peacekeeping force officer. They share a bottle of scotch.

                         COLONEL OLIVER
            The problem is, General Bizimungu,
            I have information that the
            Interahamwe militia will not heed
            the peace agreement.

                         GENERAL BIZIMUNGU
            Colonel, the UN need not worry
            about the Interahamwe. We will
            control them.

Paul arrives.

                         PAUL
            General.

                         GENERAL BIZIMUNGU
            Ah, Paul. This scotch is
            exceptional.

                         PAUL
            It is our most popular single malt.
            I knew you'd like it.

He looks at Colonel Oliver. They shake hands.

> PAUL (CONT'D)
> Colonel Oliver, it is a pleasure to
> see you, sir.

> COLONEL OLIVER
> Good to see you, Paul.

> PAUL
> General, let me recommend the
> lobster for lunch today. It is
> spectacular, straight off the
> plane.

> GENERAL BIZIMUNGU
> Fresh lobster in Kigali. You do us
> proud, Paul.

> PAUL
> Well, thank you.

> GENERAL BIZIMUNGU
> I, um, left a little something for
> you at the coat check.

> PAUL
> Excuse me, gentlemen.

Paul turns and exits.

INT. HOTEL MILLE COLLINES - STOREROOM - DAY

Paul enters the cellar, searches, finds two bottles of
whiskey.

INT. HOTEL MILLE COLLINES LOBBY - DAY

Paul arrives at the cloak room hatch, addresses the COAT
CHECK GIRL.

> PAUL
> Elizabeth, please put these in the
> General's briefcase.

Paul moves on, doing his rounds.

EXT. KIGALI STREETS - DAY

Paul speeds through the streets of Kigali. The radio plays.

> RADIO ANNOUNCER (V.O.)
> This is RTLM - Hutu power radio. I
> have a message from our President.
> Beware -- do not trust the Tutsi
> rebels. Do not shake the hand that
> will stab you. They will trick
> you...

Paul switches to another station.

> FEMALE REPORTER (V.O.)
> ...reporting from Kigali, Rwanda,
> where tensions are high, as the
> deadline for the UN-brokered peace
> agreement approaches.

EXT. PAUL'S STREET - DAY

Kids play soccer in dusty lots. Paul waves to his neighbors,
including VICTOR. He HONKS twice. The metal gate to a
fenced-off house swings open.

EXT. RUSESABAGINA HOUSE - DAY

PAUL'S OLD GUARD stands just inside. Paul waves to him and
pulls into the driveway.

> PAUL
> Hello, Jeremiah.

> JEREMIAH
> Hello, sir.

A neat bungalow and gardens are behind the high fence.

Across the garden a young man, THOMAS, and his wife, FEDENS,
play with several kids.

Paul's wife, TATIANA, a woman of great natural beauty,
emerges from the house. Beside her is ODETTE, their family
doctor and close friend.

Tatiana kisses Paul.

> PAUL
> Good evening, Odette.

Paul embraces Odette warmly.

> ODETTE
> I'll see you soon.

Odette walks away.

                    PAUL
          So your brother and the girls are
          here.

                    TATIANA
          Yes.

His brother-in-law Thomas and sister-in-law Fedens play skip
rope with the children. Paul and Tatiana walk arm in arm
toward them.

Paul's nieces ANAIS (3) and CARINE (4) are skipping rope.

                    PAUL
          Okay, Anais, let me see. Your
          turn.

Anais starts to skip rope.

                    PAUL
          Who is the winner? Oh, it doesn't
          matter. I have chocolates. Who
          wants chocolates?

                    DIANE (O.S.)
          Hey, Papa, watch this.

Two of Paul and Tatiana's four children, DIANE (8) and ELYS
(12), play in the yard.

Diane and Elys spin hula hoops around their waists.

                    PAUL
          Oh my goodness. Well, here,
          chocolates, cholates, who wants?

                    THOMAS
          Say thank you to your Uncle Paul.

                    TATIANA
          Please, not before dinner.

                    PAUL
          Not before dinner, mama says.

                    DIANE
          Thank you.

                    ELYS
          Thank you.

                        PAUL
         Okay. Let's go in.

INT. RUSESABAGINA HOUSE - LIVING ROOM - NIGHT

Paul, Thomas, and Fedens are sitting and talking. Anais and
Carine are on the floor, playing.

Tatiana carries in a tray of glasses and beers.

                        THOMAS
         Things are very slow at the shop.
         How, how are things at the hotel?

                        PAUL
         Very busy. Many people are
         visiting the gorillas. A lot of
         foreign press are arriving for the
         peace acc...

Paul and Tatiana's son ROGER (10) enters wide-eyed, afraid.

                        ROGER
         There are soldiers.

Thomas glances at Fedens.

                        PAUL
         Where?

                        ROGER
         On the street.

Paul places his beer glass onto the table and stands.

                        PAUL
         I'll go and see what's happening.
         It's all right.

EXT. RUSESABAGINA HOUSE - DRIVEWAY - NIGHT

Paul emerges, now he can hear noise.

The sounds of SPLINTERING WOOD, GLASS BREAKING, CHILDREN'S
CRIES, WOMEN SCREAMING.

Paul opens the gate slightly, peers out.

Paul *(Don Cheadle)*, center, greets Colonel Oliver *(Nick Nolte)*, right, and General Bizimungu *(Fana Mokoena)*.

The family enjoys dinner at Paul and Tatiana's house.

Blid Alshirk

Paul *(Don Cheadle)*, right, Tatiana *(Sophie Okonedo)*, and Thomas *(Antonio David Lyons)* watch their neighbor Victor get beaten and dragged into the truck by the army.

Frank Connor

Paul *(Don Cheadle)* greets Peter *(Lennox Mathabathe)*, left, David *(David O'Hara)*, and Jack *(Joaquin Phoenix)* who have arrived to cover the signing of the peace accords.

Colonel Oliver *(Nick Nolte)* toasts the signing of the Arusha Peace Accords.

Tatiana *(Sophie Okonedo)* explains to Paul *(Don Cheadle)* the President has been assassinated, Tutsi homes are being set on fire, and he is the only Hutu the neighbors trust.

The neighbors look on horrified as Roger is brought in.

Paul *(Don Cheadle),* right, struggles with the danger of bringing all the neighbors to the Diplomat Hotel.

Paul *(Don Cheadle)* looks at his family as they travel through the chaos of Kigali.

Paul sees the neighbors' homes have already been looted and burned on his street.

Terror in the streets outside the Diplomat Hotel.

The neighbors amass in the hotel lobby, looking to Paul *(Don Cheadle),* right, for direction.

Jean Jacques *(Neil McCarthy),* center, leaves Paul *(Don Cheadle)* in charge of the Mille Collines Hotel.

Pat Archer *(Cara Seymour)* needs Paul *(Don Cheadle)* to shelter the van full of orphans.

The crew interviews Colonel Oliver *(Nick Nolte)* about the limitations of "peace-keeping."

Colonel Oliver *(Nick Nolte)* is outraged by the plan to abandon the Rwandans.

Frank Connor

The orphans, friends, neighbors, and refugees look on as the convoy prepares to leave.

Blid Alsbirk

Gregoire *(Tony Kgoroge)* watches the convoy pull away.

A family snapshot. From left to right, Paul *(Don Cheadle)*, Diane *(Mathabo Pieterson)*, Elys *(Mosa Kaiser)*, Tatiana *(Sophie Okonedo)*, and Roger *(Ofentse Modiselle)*.

Frank Connor

Peter *(Lennox Mathabathe)* and Jack *(Joaquin Phoenix)* film Colonel Oliver's lieutenants fending off the Interahamwe attack on the hotel.

Frank Connor

Tatiana *(Sophie Okonedo)* and Paul *(Don Cheadle)* learn Pat *(Cara Seymour)* has not been able to find their nieces.

A relief worker *(Oorlagh George)* carries a child among the crowd of refugees.

Abandoned.

Paul *(Don Cheadle)* listens and keeps order as Oliver *(Nick Nolte)* reads the names of those who have received exit visas.

Frank Connor

Tatiana *(Sophie Okonedo)* begs Paul *(Don Cheadle)* not to leave them.

Blid Alsbirk

Colonel Oliver *(Nick Nolte)* frantically tries to protect the convoy.

Frank Connor

General Bizimungu *(Fana Mokoena)* drives into the hotel.

Blid Alsbirk

The final evacuation of all the refugees from the hotel.

The evacuation convoy moves through a mass exodus of Hutus who flee to the Congo.

The Rwandan Patriotic Front army forces the Interahamwe militias to flee.

Pat Archer *(Cara Seymour)* runs to tell Paul and Tatiana she has their nieces before the bus departs.

Pat *(Cara Seymour)* and Tatiana *(Sophie Okonedo)* search for the girls.

Paul *(Don Cheadle)* has a brief moment of peace.

EXT. VICTOR'S HOUSE - NIGHT

HE SEES: (two houses down) a group of Hutu soldiers,
clustered around Jeeps. They whisper and point. It's a
raid.

                    SOLDIER
          We know you are Tutsi.

                    VICTOR'S WIFE
          Please, sir, this is my husband.
          He's just a gardener.

                    SOLDIER
          He's been spying for the rebels.

                    VICTOR'S WIFE
          No, no, we don't know any rebels.

                    SOLDIER
          You will come with us.

                    VICTOR'S WIFE
          No, no, we are telling the truth.
          We do not know any...

EXT. RUSESABAGINA HOUSE - DRIVEWAY - NIGHT

Tatiana and Thomas crowd behind Paul.

                    TATIANA
          What is it?

                    PAUL
          Tatiana, go back in the house. You
          must go back, you mustn't be out
          here.

She looks, sees the soldiers, as they drag Victor onto the
street.

                    TATIANA
          It's Victor.

EXT. VICTOR'S HOUSE - NIGHT

VICTOR is crying, pleading, like a whipped dog.

> VICTOR
> No, captain, you see...It's not,
> it's not me. Captain, captain.

EXT. RUSESABAGINA HOUSE - DRIVEWAY - NIGHT

Paul and the others watch, horrified.

> TATIANA
> (softly)
> We, we must do something.

> VICTOR'S WIFE (O.S.)
> (sobs)
> No! No!

> SOLDIER (O.S.)
> Traitor!

> PAUL (SOFTLY)
> Do what?

> TATIANA (SOFTLY)
> Call someone.

> VICTOR (O.S.)
> I'm not going. I'm not, I'm, I'm
> not going. I'm not going.

EXT. VICTOR'S HOUSE - NIGHT

A soldier strikes Victor with a gun.

Victor loses it completely. He stops pleading, grabs onto a
soldier, clinging, screaming like a terrified child -- like a
man who knows he is going to die. It's a horror.

The soldiers beat and kick him as he's lying on the ground.

EXT. RUSESABAGINA HOUSE - DRIVEWAY - NIGHT

> TATIANA
> We must do something.

> VICTOR'S WIFE (O.S.)
> Please help him, please help him!

Paul closes the gate quickly. A soldier turns and stares at
Paul, menacing.

                    VICTOR'S WIFE (O.S.)
          Oh Victor! Victor!

Paul glances at Tatiana and Thomas.

                    PAUL
          There's nothing we can do. You
          must stay the night, Thomas.

                    THOMAS
          Yes.

                    VICTOR'S WIFE (O.S.)
          (SCREAMS) No, Victor! No!

INT. RUSESABAGINA HOUSE - TATIANA/PAUL'S BEDROOM - NIGHT

Paul lies in bed, unable to sleep. The clock reads 3:00 a.m.

                    TATIANA
          Why would they arrest Victor? He
          has no politics. He's a gardener.

                    PAUL
          Who knows. Who knows. Someone who
          didn't like him denounced him as a
          rebel spy. Happens all the time
          now.

                    TATIANA
          Maybe -- you could call one of your
          contacts in the army?

                    PAUL
          It wouldn't help.

                    TATIANA
          You could ask for a favor.

                    PAUL
          No I could not. All day long I
          work to please this officer, that
          diplomat, some tourist, to store up
          favors, so that if there is a time
          we need help, I have powerful
          people I can call upon.

                    TATIANA
          But Victor was a good neighbor.

                    PAUL
          He's not family. Family is all
          that matters. Please...please,
          leave things to my good judgement.

His turn away indicates the discussion is over.

EXT. HOTEL MILLE COLLINES - FRONT GATE - DAY

Paul drives down the hotel driveway, past the guard house.

EXT. HOTEL MILLE COLLINES - FORECOURT - DAY

The hotel entrance is busy with MINI VANS, white UN jeeps,
foreign news crew Land Rovers and a TV repair van unloading
monitors. Paul pulls up, turns over the van to the valet,
greets new arrivals.

DAVID, PETER and JACK, reporters, stand in the courtyard.

                    DAVID
          This assignment is bullshit.

                    JACK
          Come on. A few days in a nice
          hotel, no one shooting at us?

Paul walks toward the three men.

                    PAUL
          Gentlemen. Welcome to the Mille
          Collines. I am Paul Rusesabagina,
          the house manager.

                    PETER
          Hi.

Paul and Jack shake hands.

                    PAUL (CONT'D)
          Anything that you need, please find
          me.

                    DAVID
          Thank you.

INT. HOTEL MILLE COLLINES - BAR - DAY

Jack sits at the bar, talking with BENEDICT KIRANJA, a Kigali
journalist. Paul is nearby.

JACK
So, what is the actual difference
between a Hutu and a Tutsi?

BENEDICT
According to the Belgian colonists,
the Tutsis are taller and more
elegant. It was the Belgians that
created the division.

JACK
How?

BENEDICT
They picked people...those with
thinner noses, lighter skin. They
used to measure the width of
people's noses. The Belgians used
the Tutsis to run the country.
Then, when they left, they left the
power to the Hutus. And of course,
the Hutus took revenge on the elite
Tutsis for years of repression.

Behind them David, the reporter, speaks with General
Bizimungu.

BENEDICT
Am I telling the truth, Paul?

PAUL
Yes, unfortunately.

Paul hands a tray, holding a bottle of cognac, to a waiter.

PAUL (CONT'D)
Please take this to the General.

He turns back to Jack and Benedict.

PAUL (CONT'D)
Benedict is our finest journalist
in Kigali, an expert on the
subject.

JACK
So what are you, Paul?

PAUL
I am Hutu. Gentlemen.

Paul leaves and Jack turns to two attractive hookers, CHLOE
and MIRIAM, seated next.

>   JACK
>   Excuse me, honey, can I ask you a
>   personal question?

She turns to look at him.

>   JACK (CONT'D)
>   Are you a Hutu or a Tutsi?

>   CHLOE
>   (surprised)
>   I am Tutsi.

>   JACK
>   And your friend. Tutsi?

>   MIRIAM
>   No, I am Hutu.

Jack nods and turns back to Benedict.

>   JACK
>   They could be twins.

David leaves Bizimungu's table, hurries over to Jack.

>   DAVID
>   Get the camera. The General's
>   going to give us an interview.

Jack leans over to Chloe.

>   JACK
>   Hey, I'm in Room 22. I'd love to
>   finish this conversation.

INT. HOTEL MILLE COLLINES - DAVID'S ROOM - DAY

David is sitting at the edit desk, replaying his interview
with the General. He takes notes as he watches.

>   DAVID (V.O. THRU MONITOR)
>   Senior UN officers claim that the
>   Rwandan Army is secretly training
>   and arming the Hutu Militia called
>   the Interahamwe. I put this claim
>   to the head of the armed forces,
>   General Bizimungu.

We see the General on the monitor.

                    GENERAL BIZIMUNGU
          No. No, we have not been training
          the Militia. The UN are mistaken
          in this accusation.

                    DAVID
          Do you support your President's
          agreement to make peace with the
          rebels?

                    GENERAL BIZIMUNGU
          The President has the full support
          of the army.

                    DAVID
          That peace agreement will be signed
          today in Tanzania between Tutsi
          rebel forces and President
          Habyarimana.

INT. HOTEL MILLE COLLINES - FUNCTION ROOM - DAY

The reception is underway. The room is filled with staff
from various embassies, moderate Tutsi and Hutu politicians,
businessmen and journalists. Colonel Oliver is standing at a
podium, addressing the room.

                    COLONEL OLIVER
          This is a great day for Rwanda and
          for all of Africa. Negotiation has
          replaced confrontation....

                                        CUT TO:

EXT. HOTEL MILLE COLLINES - GARDEN/SWIMMING POOL

General Bizimungu sits with George Rutagunda, who is now in a
shiny blue suit. The bottle of cognac on the table is almost
gone. Bizimungu and Rutagunda watch the peace celebration.

Paul walks over to the General's table.

                    GENERAL BIZIMUNGU
          Ah, Paul. Have a drink.

                    COLONEL OLIVER (O.S.)
          Friendship has replaced fear.
          Ladies and gentlemen, we have a
          live feed to the signing of the
          peace agreement.

Paul picks up the offered glass and they toast.

> GENERAL BIZIMUNGU
> May we all find peace.

Bizimungu looks to Rutagunda, a conspiratorial glance --
something's wrong here.

INT. HOTEL MILLE COLLINES - FUNCTION ROOM - DAY

> COLONEL OLIVER
> Let us all dedicate ourselves to
> nurturing this hard-earned accord.

The Colonel raises a glass to the journalists in the room.

> COLONEL OLIVER (CONT'D)
> To peace.

EXT. HOTEL MILLE COLLINES - GROUNDS - NIGHT

Reporters and crews pack their equipment into vans. Paul
speaks with a JOURNALIST.

> JOURNALIST
> Be sure to look me up if you come
> over.

> PAUL
> Ah, yes, it is a beautiful city. I
> am planning on returning there as --

He sees Thomas and Fedens as they walk across the forecourt.

> PAUL (CONT'D)
> -- oh, forgive me.

> JOURNALIST
> Thank you. Bye.

Paul turns to Thomas and Fedens. Paul and Thomas embrace.

> PAUL
> Hello, Fedens.

Paul kisses her cheek.

> PAUL
> Well this is a surprise.

                         THOMAS
              Oh, forgive us, Paul -- we must
              talk.

                         PAUL
              Yes. What's wrong?

EXT. HOTEL MILLE COLLINES - GARDEN/SWIMMING POOL - NIGHT

Tiki torches, feeling of tranquility. Barbecue blazes.
Drinks are served at a table as Paul listens to Thomas.

                         THOMAS
              I have it from a very reliable
              source, Paul.

                         PAUL
              Who?

                         THOMAS
              He's...

A waiter carries a tray with some drinks. Paul takes the
tray from him.

                         PAUL
              Thank you, Stephen.

Thomas waits to speak until the waiter is out of earshot.

                         THOMAS
              My assistant -- the Hutu Power man.
              He says that we must get out now,
              that soon it'll be very bad.

Paul stifles his anger.

                         PAUL
              Give me this man's name.

                         THOMAS
              But please, Paul, even though he is
              Interahamwe...he's a friend.

                         PAUL
              He wants your job, Thomas.

                         THOMAS
              He said -- that there is a signal.
              It is "Cut the tall trees." And
              when they hear this signal, the
              militia are to go to war.

> FEDENS
> Paul, please, let us take Tatiana
> with us. You are Hutu, you will be
> safe.

> PAUL
> Fedens...I know you have heard many
> things. And I know what we have
> seen, Thomas, but please, the
> United Nations are here now. The
> world press are watching. The
> peace has been signed, let this
> process work.

Suddenly the lights go out all over the hotel and it is dark.
Then they flicker and come back on as the generator kicks in.

> FEDENS
> What was that?

> PAUL
> It's power cuts. We are running on
> generators. Fedens, please don't
> worry.

He turns to Thomas.

> PAUL (CONT'D)
> Tomorrow you will come by the
> house, and we will discuss this
> with Tatiana. All right?

EXT. HOTEL MILLE COLLINES - FORECOURT - NIGHT

Paul escorts Fedens and Thomas to their car.

> THOMAS
> Goodnight, Paul.

> PAUL
> Yes. Kiss the girls for me.

EXT. KIGALI STREETS - NIGHT

Paul's at the wheel, driving. Barely a car on the road.
Shadows dart past faint lights. A house is on fire. A
scream in the night.

Shadows dart across the flames.

Paul switches the preset buttons on the radio as he drives.
He can only find fevered drum-based MUSIC.

An army jeep and an Interahamwe truck, without lights on,
roar out of the darkness.

> SOLDIER
> Stay in your houses! Stay in your
> houses! Everybody stay in your
> house!

EXT. PAUL'S GARDEN - NIGHT

Paul pulls up at his house, it is in darkness.

EXT. RUSESABAGINA HOUSE - NIGHT

Paul emerges from the van, flashlight in hand. He walks to
the door.

INT. RUSESABAGINA HOUSE - LIVING ROOM - NIGHT

Paul steps in quietly, tries the light switch, nothing. He
listens. The beam of his flashlight cuts the blackness.

> PAUL
> Tatiana?

INT. RUSESABAGINA HOUSE - HALL - NIGHT

Paul continues his search. Shines his light into a room.
Looks for a second, then closes the door and walks to the
next. He stops and listens with his ear to the door.
Nothing. He pushes it in.

INT. RUSESABAGINA HOUSE - PAUL/TATIANA'S BEDROOM - NIGHT

Paul's light sweeps across the room and illuminates EYES --
terrified eyes. A room full of faces, staring back.

From among the faces, Tatiana's voice comes, heavy with
relief. She is holding Diane.

> TATIANA
> Paul.

> PAUL
> Tatiana.

Paul's eyes adjust. He recognizes many of his neighbors, all crowded into this small room. Then he sees their friends Odette and her husband Jean Baptiste.

> JEAN BAPTISTE
> Paul.

> PAUL
> What is going on here?

> JEAN BAPTISTE
> Our house has been burned.

> PAUL
> What?

> ODETTE
> Didn't you hear the news?

> PAUL
> What, what, what news?

> TATIANA
> They are saying President
> Habyrimana has been murdered.

> ODETTE
> Tutsi rebels have killed him.

> PAUL
> Nonsense. Why would the rebels
> kill the President when he agreed
> to peace?

Paul is shocked but tries to pull things together.

> PAUL (CONT'D)
> Everyone, please, out of this room,
> please. Jean Baptiste, find them
> seats in the other room.

> TATIANA
> Did you meet with Thomas and
> Fedens?

> PAUL
> Yes, I told them to go home. Go
> and call them, Tatsi.

Tatiana shakes her head no.

> TATIANA
> I've tried. Our phones, they do
> not work.

> PAUL
> Why do the neighbors run to us?

> TATIANA
> You are the only Hutu they can
> trust.

> PAUL
> You are Tutsi.

> TATIANA
> They are so scared, Paul. I am
> scared.

He hugs her.

> PAUL
> These are probably rumors started
> by agitators. We must remain calm
> for the children, Tatsi.

Odette peeks back into the room. Elys is with her.

> ODETTE
> Forgive me, Paul. Elys says that
> Roger has gone.

> TATIANA
> Gone! Gone where?

> ELYS
> He was afraid for his friend Simon,
> Mama.

> PAUL
> Where has he gone, Elys!

> ELYS
> He went next door.

EXT. RUSESABAGINA HOUSE - GARDEN - NIGHT

Along the darkened driveway, a flashlight beam moves along
the bushes.

> TATIANA
> Paul, wait. (pause) Paul.

> PAUL
> Tatiana, go back inside!

> TATIANA
> Please, please. I just want to,
> please...

> PAUL
> You'll stay in the house. No.

Paul crawls through the bushes. Roger is hidden among the branches.

> ROGER
> AAHH.

In the bushes, Roger is curled up on the ground, crying. He is covered with blood.

> TATIANA (O.S.)
> Oh, Paul, please, please, what is
> wrong?

> PAUL
> Oh no -- oh my God.

Paul pushes the branches aside and pulls Roger out.

> PAUL (CONT'D)
> Oh, my son, where are you hurt?

> TATIANA
> Is he okay? Oh, my baby.

He carries Roger in his arms and climbs from the bushes.

INT. RUSESABAGINA HOUSE - KITCHEN - NIGHT

Tatiana rushes into the kitchen and pushes dishes from the table as Paul enters, carrying Roger.

> PAUL
> Odette! Odette!

He places Roger on the table as Odette and Elys run in, followed by several of the neighbors.

> ODETTE
> Get his clothes off.

> PAUL
> He's hurt.

> ODETTE
> Tatsi, please get some water.
> Please.

> PAUL
> He's hurt.

> ODETTE
> Please, please. Let's get his
> clothes off.

The neighbors are all now gathered at the door of the
kitchen. Paul wipes blood from his son's face.

> NEIGHBOR
> He's covered in blood.

> PAUL
> Lay back, son.

> NEIGHBOR
> He went next door to the Chirangas.

> PAUL (TO ROGER)
> Shh. Shh.

Paul raises Roger's arms, one at a time, so Odette can look
for the wound. She wipes blood from it.

> ODETTE
> Stay still, Roger.

> PAUL
> Look here, look here.

> ODETTE
> Keep him still, Paul. I can't find
> the wound.

Tatiana leans over her son.

> TATIANA
> Roger, what happened to you?

> PAUL
> Tell your mother what happened,
> Roger.

Paul wipes Roger's face. The child is too terrified to
speak.

> PAUL (CONT'D)
> Shh. Roger, you're okay.

                    ODETTE
Do not worry, he is not cut. He is
not hurt. This is not his blood,
Paul.

                    PAUL (TO ROGER)
You are not cut.

                    TATIANA
My darling, it's okay. It's okay.

Paul turns to Elys, who's been standing in the doorway with
the neighbors.

                    PAUL
Come here, Elys.

                    NEIGHBOR
Where did the blood come from?

                    PAUL
Please, please. (to Roger) You
are safe.

EXT. KIGALI - DAY

Gunfire and explosions. Across the city, smoke rises from
burning buildings.

EXT. RUSESABAGINA HOUSE - TATIANA/PAUL'S BEDROOM - DAY

Elyse and Diane sleep. Tatiana is seated nearby with Roger
on her lap. Paul enters the room and walks to Tatiana. He
places his hand on Roger's shoulder and Roger flinches.

                    PAUL
          Oh, son.

                    ODETTE (O.S.)
          Paul.

EXT. RUSESABAGINA HOUSE - HALLWAY - DAY

Paul steps out of his room. The hallway is crowded. Jean
Baptiste is holding a tiny radio.

                    RADIO PRESENTER (V.O. - THRU RADIO)
          Listen to me, good people of
          Rwanda. Terrible news.

                    JEAN BAPTISTE
It is true.

                RADIO PRESENTER (V.O. - THRU RADIO)
Horrible news. Our great President
is murdered by the Tutsi
cockroaches. They tricked him to
sign their phony peace agreement.
Then they shot his plane from the
sky. It is time to clear the
brush, good Hutus of Rwanda. We
must cut the tall trees. Cut the
tall trees now!

As they listen, a young woman lets out a cry from the other
room.

                  WOMAN (O.S.)
The soldiers are here!

Women and children push toward the bedroom. Paul tries to
quiet them.

                    PAUL
Stay calm and be quiet.

EXT. RUSESABAGINA HOUSE - GARDEN - DAY

Two jeeps, jammed with heavily armed SOLDIERS, sit in the
drive like many-limbed beasts of war. Paul watches as the
jeeps rumble into his garden. The soldiers jump out. The
Hutu Captain gives orders to his men.

                  HUTU CAPTAIN
You two, check the back. Go and
find him.

INT. RUSESABAGINA HOUSE - BEDROOM - DAY

Paul watches from a window.

                    PAUL
I...I better go have a word with
them.

EXT. RUSESABAGINA HOUSE - DRIVEWAY - DAY

Paul steps out of the house, closes the door behind him.

> PAUL
> Who's in charge here?

Paul walks to the officer. A soldier kicks in the door, soldiers pour inside.

> PAUL
> Can I help you, sir?

> SOLDIER (O.S.)
> Everybody out, out, out!

> HUTU CAPTAIN
> Let me see your identity card.

Paul reaches into his pocket and removes his identity card. He hands it to the Captain.

> PAUL
> I am a good friend of General
> Bizimungu.

CLOSE ON: Paul's identity card -- it reads Ethnicity: HUTU

Soldiers force his family and neighbors into the yard. Tatiana is carrying Roger.

The captain studies Paul, waves for the soldiers to back off.

> HUTU CAPTAIN
> You work at the Hotel Diplomat?

> PAUL
> No. I work at the Mille Collines.

The Captain looks confused, angry. Paul speaks quickly.

> PAUL (CONT'D)
> I used to work at the Diplomat.

> HUTU CAPTAIN
> We want to use that hotel. All the
> room keys are in the safe. You
> must open it.

He takes Paul's arm.

> HUTU CAPTAIN (CONT'D)
> Let's go.

> TATIANA
> Paul.

                         PAUL
          Sir, I, I, I cannot leave my
          family. I must take them with me.
          It is not safe here. There are,
          there are Tutsi spies everywhere.

Paul hurries back and grabs Tatiana. Tatiana grabs Odette,
the neighbors follow.

                         HUTU CAPTAIN
          I cannot take all these people!

                         TATIANA
          No, no, sir, you do not have to.
          We, we have our own car, and our
          van.

The Captain doubtful, then his two-way radio barks - an
urgent message. He listens.

                         SOLDIER (V.O. - THRU RADIO)
          Captain Caruso, come in. Captain,
          come on.

The Captain, distracted, gives in to Paul's request.

                         HUTU CAPTAIN
          Let's go. (INTO RADIO) We found
          him. Let's go, let's go.

Tatiana drags the kids and ushers everyone toward the van.
In a second they are all clambering in.

                         PAUL
          Come on. Hurry, quick.

                         TATIANA
          Get into the van...

                         JEREMIAH
          Can I go with you?

                         PAUL
          Yes, of course, Jeremiah. Go
          round, hurry.

Paul ushers the old guard into the van and closes the doors.
He jumps behind the wheel of the van. Neighbors are jammed
in like sardines, 15, more, inside. Tatiana and their kids
are squashed together on the front bench.

The convoy (jeep - van, car - jeep) starts up and turns out
onto the street.

EXT. PAUL'S STREET - DAY

As they pass the Carigna home, there are bodies scattered
over the garden -- one is the neighbor, SIMON.

> FEMALE NEIGHBOR
> Oh, Jesus, no.

> ELYS
> Oh, it's Simon, Papa.

> PAUL
> Don't look, don't look, Tatiana.

EXT. KIGALI STREETS - DAY

The convoy speeds through the streets. Slowing only to
maneuver through makeshift roadblocks where Militia wave
machetes, nailed clubs and spears as they dance.

EXT. HOTEL DIPLOMAT - ENTRANCE - DAY

A block of flats. Several shops are being looted by the
Interahamwe. A group of Tutsis sit on the ground, terrified.

The convoy pulls up to this older, shabbier hotel.

Paul jumps out of the van, hurries to the Hutu Captain.

> PAUL
> The safe is in the manager's
> office.

The Captain points at two soldiers.

> HUTU CAPTAIN
> You two, go with him.

INT. HOTEL DIPLOMAT - MANAGER'S OFFICE - DAY

Paul bursts into the room. The two soldiers follow.

The safe is hidden behind a bookshelf. Paul spins the
combination.

One soldier sees a fridge, opens it. Inside are beers and
chocolate.

                         1ST SOLDIER
           Hey, look at this. Beer.

Paul tries the safe. It opens.

Inside he sees a big bunch of keys, a wad of dollars, Rwandan
francs, a check book and several bottles of the best cognac,
whiskey, some Cristal.

Paul leans toward the safe to pick up the room keys. As
their attention is diverted Paul reaches in, grabs the money.

Paul opens the jewelry box as the soldier looks over.

                         2ND SOLDIER
           Hey, hey, hey.

Paul glances at the soldiers, closes the jewelry box, picks
up the room keys, gestures. Closes the safe.

                         PAUL
           I've got them.

INT. HOTEL DIPLOMAT - ENTRANCE - DAY

Paul emerges to see that his van is now empty. He rushes
around it and sees all of the occupants of the van, Tatiana,
his kids, Odette, on their knees with their hands over their
heads.

The Captain hovers over them, pistol in hand.

                         HUTU CAPTAIN
           Get down, all of you.

                         PAUL (SOFTLY)
           Sir, sir. Here, I have them, I
           have them, I've got them.

The Captain turns, sees Paul. He marches toward Paul and
knocks the keys from his hands, then SLAPS HIM HARD on the
face.

                         TATIANA
           No!

                         HUTU CAPTAIN
           Traitor!

Paul reels from the blow, but somehow manages to stay on his
feet. The Captain snatches a bunch of identification cards
from a soldier, hurls the cards in Paul's face.

> HUTU CAPTAIN
> These are Tutsi cockroaches!

> PAUL
> Let me explain, sir. Please!
> Wait!

The Captain grabs Paul by the scruff of the neck, pushes him toward the kneeling captives. The Captain snatches a pistol from one of his soldiers, shoves it into Paul's hand, gestures to the group.

> HUTU CAPTAIN
> Shoot them!

Paul looks at him.

> HUTU CAPTAIN (CONT'D)
> Shoot them!

> PAUL
> Please, I...I don't use guns.

> HUTU CAPTAIN
> It's easy.

The Captain raises his own pistol and FIRES it.

> HUTU CAPTAIN (CONT'D)
> Shoot them or you die first.

The Captain aims his pistol at Paul's head.

> PAUL
> Sir...What could I pay you not to
> do this?

The Captain laughs.

> HUTU CAPTAIN
> You wanna pay me?

> PAUL
> Why not? Look at them.

He gestures to the neighbors.

> PAUL (CONT'D)
> These are not rebels. Soon they
> will be worthless to you. Why not
> take some money for your work?

> HUTU CAPTAIN
> How much?

> PAUL
> You name a price.

> HUTU CAPTAIN
> Ten thousand francs for each.

> PAUL
> Sir, I don't have that much.

> HUTU CAPTAIN
> Okay.

The Captain laughs, snatches the gun from Paul, marches toward them.

> PAUL
> Wait, wait, wait.

Paul reaches into his pocket, pulls out a bunch of dollars.

> PAUL (CONT'D)
> Here. It's a thousand, a thousand
> US. And here.

Paul wets his finger and removes his ring.

> PAUL (CONT'D)
> Fifty thousand francs for my wife
> and children.

> HUTU CAPTAIN
> Get them.

The Hutu Captain nods and Paul runs over, grabs Tatiana, Roger, the three girls.

> TATIANA
> Go, go.

Paul ushers Tatiana out. As Tatiana stands, she takes Odette's arm.

> TATIANA
> Come, Odette, please.

> PAUL (TO ODETTE)
> Have you any money?

> ODETTE
> Nothing.

                    HUTU CAPTAIN
          Hey.

The Hutu Captain gestures toward Paul and Odette with his
pistol. Paul sees the Captain pocket the dollars, move
toward the line.

                    TATIANA
          Paul, don't let them die, please.

                    PAUL
          Shh. Get in. Get in the van.

He pushes her into the van, digs into his soul for all the
courage he can muster, then turns back to the General.

                    PAUL (CONT'D)
          Sir -- I, I have more money,
          actually.

Paul reaches into his pocket and takes out his wallet, then
removes his watch and hands it to the Captain.

                    PAUL (CONT'D)
          And let them give you something,
          some money, whatever they have.
          (TO NEIGHBORS) Give me everything
          you have.

A pathetic rain of Rwandan francs, useless coins, watches,
jewelry falls into Paul's hands.

He takes the jewelry and other items and hands them to the
Captain.

                    PAUL
          Here you are. See?

The Captain looks at it, then:

                    HUTU CAPTAIN
          This is enough for one cockroach.
          Pick one.

The Captain raises his pistol. Now each terrified neighbor
looks to Paul, begging. The Captain points the gun.

                    PAUL
          Sir. I will give you a hundred
          thousand francs for all of them.

                    HUTU CAPTAIN
          Give me it.

The Captain points the gun.

>   PAUL
> I don't have it here. At the Mille
> Collines I can get it for you.

>   HUTU CAPTAIN
> You will run into the hotel and
> hide behind the UN.

>   PAUL
> Sir, I swear. One hundred thousand
> francs. I will get you the money.
> You keep them outside. Please sir.
> Please.

The Captain smiles.

>   HUTU CAPTAIN
> Let's go.

>   PAUL
> Everyone in the van. Quickly,
> quickly.

He ushers everyone back into the van.

EXT. HOTEL MILLE COLLINES - FRONT GATE - DAY

The convoy pulls up at the outer gates of the Mille Collines.
It's armed by FOUR ARMED UN PEACEKEEPERS.

The Captain walks to Paul in the van.

>   HUTU CAPTAIN
> Go with my soldiers. And hurry
> back if you want to keep these
> cockroaches.

EXT. HOTEL MILLE COLLINES - FORECOURT - DAY

Chaos -- UN jeeps, hotel vans, elite Tutsi refugees checking
in.

INT. HOTEL MILLE COLLINES - LOBBY - DAY

Paul rushes in. The lobby is filled with Tutsi refugees and
scared white tourists.

A solitary receptionist is besieged by anxious guests.

She sees Paul.

                    RECEPTIONIST (CON'T)
          Excuse me, sir. Please could you --

Paul rushes past to the manager's office, closes the door.

INT. HOTEL MILLE COLLINES - MANAGER'S OFFICE - DAY

Paul crouches by the cupboard, opening it to find the safe.
He unlocks the safe, opens the door and removes wads of
banknotes.

EXT. HOTEL MILLE COLLINES - FRONT GATE - DAY

Paul climbs out of the soldiers' jeep. He hurries around
toward the Hutu Captain and hands him the banknotes.

                    PAUL
          Here's the money. One hundred
          thousand francs as promised. Now
          please let them go, sir.

No response. Money in hand, the Captain eyes Paul with
malice.

                    SOLDIER (O.S.)
          Take the money. We will get them
          later.

                    HUTU CAPTAIN
          You can go.

                    PAUL
          Thank you.

                    HUTU CAPTAIN
          Traitor.

The Captain smiles, then jumps in his jeep and speeds off.
Paul runs to the van and jumps in. Odette is in tears.

                    ODETTE
          Thank you, Paul.

Paul doesn't reply. Tatiana hugs him. He gives her a look -
a mix of relief and anger.

EXT. HOTEL MILLE COLLINES - FORECOURT - DAY

Paul's van pulls up at the valet desk. Jean Jacques is at
another van, talking to Dube, who is standing outside.

> JEAN JACQUES
> You must tell him when he comes...

Dube sees Paul getting out of his van.

> DUBE
> Here he is, sir.

Paul hurries over.

> JEAN JACQUES
> Paul. I have to go. The staff of
> Kivu Lodge have fled. I have to
> close up there. You are in charge
> now.

He flings office keys to Paul and his van takes off.

INT. HOTEL MILLE COLLINES - LOBBY - DAY

At the reception desk the same receptionist is overwhelmed.

Paul leads his group through the lobby.

> PAUL
> Come on. Can everyone please move
> to the side. Clear the door.
> Come, Tatsi, come.

He waves to ANDRE, one of the hotel employees.

> PAUL (CONT'D)
> I need two suites.

Several guests crowd about Paul, overwhelming him with
questions.

> 1ST FEMALE GUEST
> Paul, please, where is my passport?

> 2ND FEMALE GUEST
> Paul, oh, thank goodness.

Andre hands keys to Paul.

                    PAUL
          If you give me one moment, please.

He turns and hands keys to Tatiana and Odette.

                    TATIANA
          What about our neighbors? What
          will they do?

Paul spots Dube, summons him over.

                    PAUL
          Dube.

                    DUBE
          Yes, sir?

                    PAUL
          Dube, please, um, put these guests
          into staff rooms.

                    DUBE
          Right away, sir.

INT. HOTEL MILLE COLLINES - PAUL'S ROOM - DAY

Paul carries Roger and leads his family into a one-bedroom
suite. The beds are unmade, towels are on the floor and the
remains of a meal sit on the dining table. The girls hurry
to the table and move to eat from the plate of leftovers.

                    TATIANA
          No, please. It's old. Have the
          fruit.

She picks apples from a fruit bowl.

Paul lays Roger onto the bed.

                    PAUL
          It's all right, Roger.

He removes Roger's shoes, looks toward the valet, who is
clutching a suit in his arms.

                    PAUL (CONT'D)
          Ah, Joseph.

                    VALET
          Your suit, sir.

                    PAUL
          This mess is unacceptable. Call
          housekeeping, get them up here
          right away.

                    VALET
          Yes, sir.

                    PAUL
          Thank you.

Tatiana sits on the bed, and picks up the phone to dial.

                    TATIANA
          I'm trying Thomas and Fedens.

                    PAUL
          All right.

INT. HOTEL MILLE COLLINES - PAUL'S BATHROOM - DAY

Paul looks in the mirror, examines his bruised face.

                    TATIANA (O.S.)
          Hello? Operator, I need a line. I
          need a line now. Please. Hello?

INT. HOTEL MILLE COLLINES - PAUL'S ROOM - DAY

Paul steps back into the room and pulls on his suit jacket.

                    PAUL
          You did not reach them?

                    TATIANA
              (Fearful)
          No.

                    PAUL
          I will send someone for them.

INT. HOTEL MILLE COLLINES - BAR - DAY

Families are gathered around listening to a radio.

                    PRESIDENT CLINTON (V.O. - THRU RADIO)
          It is a very tense situation, and I
          just want to assure the families of
          those who are there that we are
          doing everything we possibly can to
          ensure the safety of our citizens
          there.

INT. HOTEL MILLE COLLINES - LOBBY - DAY

Paul is besieged by anxious guests.

                    2ND FEMALE GUEST
          Can you at least tell us is the
          airport open?

                    PAUL
          We are calling the airport. We are
          calling the Embassy. We are trying
          to get as much information for you
          as we can.

He turns to another guest.

                    PAUL (CONT'D)
          And yes, your passport, Antoinette
          will take care of this for you.
          Dube, where is Gregoire?

Dube pauses as guests rush by.

                    DUBE
          Sir, he has moved into the
          presidential suite.

Paul storms off.

INT. HOTEL MILLE COLLINES - HALLWAY - DAY

Paul arrives at a door with a placard reading "PRESIDENTIAL
SUITE." He knocks. The door opens. Gregoire answers,
wearing a bathrobe.

                    GREGOIRE
          Ah...Mr. Manager.

                    PAUL
          What do you think you are doing,
          Gregoire?

A woman appears behind him.

                    GREGOIRE'S GIRLFRIEND
          Who is it?

                    GREGOIRE
          It's okay, darling.

He turns to Paul.

                    GREGOIRE (CONT'D)
          What do you want?

                    PAUL
          You had better get out of this room
          and back downstairs right away.

                    GREGOIRE
          I don't have to listen to you
          anymore.

                    PAUL
          Yes you do. I am in charge, now
          get out of this room right now.

                    GREGOIRE
          Mr. Manager...do you notice the
          smell of cockroaches? If I were to
          leave this room, I'm sure I could
          find it. And I know people who can
          cleanse it. (STARES) But maybe
          that doesn't bother you. Why is
          that? Are you used to the smell?
          Well, not me. I need a clean room
          to escape it.

Gregoire closes the door. Paul's eyes burn with anger, but
this battle will have to wait.

EXT. HOTEL MILLE COLLINES - FORECOURT - DAY

A RED CROSS VAN pulls up to the valet.

Guests and Tutsi refugees are everywhere.

                    HOTEL WORKER
          Please move into the hotel.
          Everyone, keep moving.

A TUTSI MAN stops Paul.

                    TUTSI MAN
          My house has been burned. I have
          nowhere to go.

                         PAUL
         Yes, I understand this, your Honor.
         But we are operating at capacity as
         it is. I can give you one room,
         but you will have to share it.

The Red Cross volunteer, PAT ARCHER, calls out to Paul.

                         PAT ARCHER
         Paul.

Paul turns toward Pat.

                         PAUL
         Yes?

                         PAT ARCHER
         Paul, I need your help.

She takes his hand.

                         PAUL
         Yes, Madame Archer.

She leads him out to her Red Cross van.

EXT. HOTEL MILLE COLLINES - FORECOURT - DAY

The sliding door of a Red Cross van pulls open to reveal
young orphans, 20 of them, from 3 - 12. They all sit, wide-
eyed with fear.

Pat sees the look of shock on Paul's face.

                         PAT ARCHER
         They're Tutsi children from the St.
         Francis orphanage. Okay, come on,
         let's go.

                         PAUL
         I have only one room.

                         PAT ARCHER
         That'll do.

Pat urges them out of the van. They are silent, totally
obedient.

Paul waves to a hotel worker.

                         PAUL
         Otto, please.

The orphans line up as UN soldiers usher refugees in the
background.

Pat looks at the orphans and closes the van cargo door.

> PAT ARCHER
> Have to go get the rest of them.

> PAUL
> The rest of them?

> PAT ARCHER
> There are another ten. I'll be
> back soon.

She gets into the van. Paul is speechless. He's just been
dumped with 20 orphans. As Pat is about to drive off, Paul
stops her.

> PAUL
> Madame Archer.

She stops.

> PAUL (CONT'D)
> I need a favor, please.

She can hardly refuse.

> PAUL (CONT'D)
> My brother-in-law and his family.
> They live close by the St. Francis.
> On O'Clare, twenty. Can you please
> get them, and, and, bring them here
> to me?

He scribbles the address.

> PAT ARCHER
> Sure.

> PAUL
> And I have a photo.

He hands her a photograph of Fedens and Thomas clutching
Anais and Carine.

> PAT ARCHER
> Thanks, Paul.

> PAUL
> Thank you.

The van pulls away and Paul watches the last of the orphans
as they are led in.

INT. HOTEL MILLE COLLINES - PAUL'S ROOM - NIGHT

Paul walks into the room. Tatiana kisses him. Roger is on
the bed.

> PAUL
> Has he spoken to you yet?

> TATIANA
> No.

> PAUL
> No.

He kisses Roger's head, falls back on the bed. Tatiana lies
on top of him.

> TATIANA
> Is your face still hurting?

> PAUL
> It's all right.

> TATIANA
> The neighbors asked me to thank you
> for your kindness.

> PAUL
> I shouldn't have brought them here.
> The first thing they told me when I
> received my appointment was to
> never, never lower the tone of the
> hotel. "Maintain the Mille
> Collines' dignity at all times,
> Paul." Soon all of this will be
> over. What if I lose my job,
> Tatiana? Oh. Oh my God.

Paul jumps up.

> TATIANA
> Where are you going?

> PAUL
> I'll be right back.

He runs out of the room.

INT. HOTEL MILLE COLLINES - ORPHANS' ROOM - NIGHT

The door of a hotel room opens, light filters in.

Paul discovers all of the orphans sitting around the room in the dark. All awake, all in total silence, fearful eyes staring at the door.

ALICE the waitress arrives as Paul turns on a light.

> PAUL
> Take care of them.

> ALICE
> How, sir?

> PAUL
> Bathe them -- feed them -- put them to bed.

He hands her the room key.

> PAUL (CONT'D)
> I will send you some help.

Alice turns toward the children as Paul leaves.

> ALICE
> Okay, babies.

EXT. HOTEL MILLE COLLINES - GROUNDS - DAY

Colonel Oliver's being interviewed by the reporter David. Gunfire crackles in the background.

> DAVID
> We have heard reports of reprisal massacres. Will the UN intervene to stop the bloodshed?

> COLONEL OLIVER
> We're here as peace keepers, not peace makers. My orders are not to intervene. Excuse me.

Colonel Oliver shakes David's hand, moves off. David talks to his cameraman.

> DAVID
> Okay. You get it?

                    JACK
          It was fine. Listen, I've got us a
          car, but we've gotta move now.

                    DAVID
          We're not allowed to do that, Jack.

                    JACK
          David, the shit's going down
          outside these walls. We've gotta
          cover it.

                    DAVID
          We're not leaving the hotel grounds
          unless we have an armored car,
          that's the ground rules.

                    JACK
          Oh, the ground rules? Where do you
          think we are, Wimbledon?

                    DAVID
          We cover the story from here until
          we get the proper vehicles, Jack.
          Shoot some "B" roll of the
          refugees.

He walks off. Jack waits 'til he's gone, then turns to
Peter, nods to the car.

                    JACK
          Let's go.

Paul and Colonel Oliver talk.

                    PAUL
          Colonel, I have no way to protect
          these people. And I have more
          refugees than I have room for as it
          is. I was given twenty orphans
          today by the Red Cross. This is
          not a refugee camp -- can you not
          take them with you to your
          facilities?

                    COLONEL OLIVER
          No, I can't do that, Paul. I'm
          sorry. I'm overwhelmed at my
          refuge camp. I'm under constant
          attack. As soon as we can
          stabilize the situation, I'll take
          'em. Okay?

Oliver walks away.

INT. HOTEL MILLE COLLINES - KITCHEN - DAY

Paul enters the empty kitchen. He discovers all the cooks
and kitchen staff listening to the radio.

>   RADIO ANNOUNCER (V.O. - THRU RADIO)
>   ...and stop the Tutsi cockroaches
>   who try to run from justice. The
>   Tutsi cockroach judge called Makesa
>   is hiding at 4 Rue De Vendun and
>   the traitor Kabulla and his
>   cockroaches --

Paul angrily throws dishes in a sink.

>   PAUL
>   Turn that radio off.

>   RADIO ANNOUNCER (V.O. - THRU RADIO)
>   -- are trying to escape in a new
>   Mercedes. Watch out for him. He --

The Head Chef switches off the radio.

>   PAUL
>   And get back to work. We have a
>   hotel to run.

>   HEAD CHEF
>   There is no work here anymore. The
>   boss has left.

>   PAUL
>   I am your boss.

Smirks and laughs among the cooks, Paul turns and leaves.

INT. SABENA OFFICES - BELGIUM - TILLEN'S OFFICE - DAY

Sabena President TILLENS at his desk.

>   SECRETARY (THROUGH SPEAKER PHONE)
>   Sir, there's a call from the Mille
>   Collines in Rwanda on line one.

Tillens leans against the desk and presses a button on the
speaker phone.

                    TILLENS
          Yes -- who am I speaking to?

INT. HOTEL MILLE COLLINES - MANAGER'S OFFICE - DAY

Paul is seated at the Manager's desk, on the phone.

                    PAUL (V.O - THRU SPEAKER PHONE)
          Yes, sir, Paul Rusesabagina, the
          house manager. I met you on your
          last visit here, Mr. Tillens.

INT. SABENA OFFICES - BELGIUM - TILLEN'S OFFICE - DAY

Tillens speaks into the speaker phone.

                    TILLENS
          Ah, yes. Paul, I remember. How
          are things there?

                    PAUL (V.O. - THRU SPEAKER PHONE)
          The situation is difficult, sir.

                    TILLENS
          Some of our directors believe we
          should close the Mille Collines
          until this unrest is over. I'm not
          sure about that, Paul. What do you
          think?

INT. HOTEL MILLE COLLINES - MANAGER'S OFFICE - DAY

This is really bad news. Paul can't allow them to close.

                    PAUL
          Sir, that would be very bad for our
          reputation. The Mille Collines is
          an oasis of calm for all our loyal
          customers. What would they think
          if Sabena deserted them now? I
          assure you, the United Nations have
          everything under control, sir.

Gunfire in the background.

INT. SABENA OFFICES - BELGIUM - TILLEN'S OFFICE - DAY

The President looks at the others.

> TILLENS
> Very well, Paul, very well. But if
> this thing gets worse, we must
> close. If there is anything I can
> do, please call.

> PAUL (V.O. - THRU SPEAKER PHONE)
> Sir, yes, there is one thing I'm
> going to be needing from you right
> away.

INT. HOTEL MILLE COLLINES - MANAGER'S OFFICE - LATER

Paul waits by the fax machine, then it spits out a single
page.

INT. HOTEL MILLE COLLINES - FUNCTION ROOM - DAY

Every member of the staff is gathered together. Paul
addresses them.

> PAUL
> Most of us in this room know each
> other and worked together for many
> years. Is it really necessary for
> me to get a letter from Belgium for
> you to perform your duties?

He holds up the fax from Belgium.

> PAUL (CONT'D)
> In fact...

He crushes the fax.

> PAUL (CONT'D)
> ...forget this letter. If you
> don't want to work for me and would
> rather be out there, then leave
> now.

The staff stare at one another. No one moves.

> PAUL (CONT'D)
> Please, everyone -- back to work.

INT. HOTEL MILLE COLLINES - DAVID'S ROOM - DAY

The blinds are drawn, we don't know whether it is day or
night.

David is editing together some of his clips. On the monitor
we see film of the refugees arriving at the hotel. Colonel
Oliver being interviewed.

A knock, Paul enters along with a waiter carrying a tray of
neatly cut sandwiches and a pot of tea.

> DAVID
> Paul, thank you for coming.

> PAUL
> Yes.

> DAVID
> The air conditioner's on the blink.
> Is there any way you could have a
> look at it? I'm just on a
> deadline.

> PAUL
> Certainly.

> DAVID
> Thank you.

Paul crouches down to check it.

> DAVID (O.S. - INTO PHONE)
> Fred, let me know when you get the
> satellite feed. Thanks.

> PAUL
> Mr. Fleming, I brought you some tea
> as well, sir.

> DAVID
> Thank you, Paul. You're an oasis
> in a desert.

On the monitor, David's interview with Colonel Oliver is
playing.

> COLONEL OLIVER (V.O. THRU MONITOR)
> The elements in the government and
> army are following the example of
> what happened to the Americans in
> Somalia. I think they intend to
> intimidate us, try to attack and
> hope that the West will pull all
> its troops out.

> DAVID (V.O. THRU MONITOR)
> Do you think they'll succeed?

> COLONEL OLIVER (V.O. THRU MONITOR)
> No, they won't. The UN's here to
> stay.

> DAVID (V.O. THRU MONITOR)
> What about the outbreak of violence
> since the shooting down of the
> President's plane...

The door opens and Jack walks in, clutching the camera.
Peter follows behind. David is furious.

> DAVID
> What the hell do you think you're
> doing?

Jack ignores her and removes the cassette from the camera.

> DAVID (CONT'D)
> I'm responsible for the safety of
> this crew.

Jack moves to the cassette player and inserts the tape. He
hits play. They watch the monitor.

> DAVID (CONT'D)
> What is this?

Now Jack realizes that Paul is in the room. He is
embarrassed at what Paul is about to see. He leaves.

On the monitor: blurry focus of a shanty town on a hill.

NOW FOCUS: A crowd hovering close to a group of Rwandan
Tutsis seated on the ground. Two Militia emerge from the
crowd, waving machetes. They SLASH their way along the line,
savage, powerful blows.

> DAVID (CONT'D)
> Where did you get this?

> PETER
> Half a mile down the road.

On screen: the crowd runs off, waving machetes. David
snatches up the phone, dials.

> DAVID (INTO PHONE)
> Fred, it's David. I've got
> incredible footage. It's a
> massacre. Dead bodies, machetes.
> (MORE)

DAVID (INTO PHONE) (cont'd)
If I get this through right away,
could you make the evening news?
Yeah. You have to lead with this.

Paul continues to watch the massacre. He is stunned.

EXT. HOTEL MILLE COLLINES - GARDENS/POOL - NIGHT

A waiter carries drinks to a table where Jack and Peter sit
with two attractive hookers. One is Chloe.

JACK
I point at you, you do a shot.

Jack spots Paul, as he adjusts a door.

PAUL
Excuse me, Mr. Daglish.

JACK
Hey, Paul. Listen. Sorry about
earlier. If I'd have known you
were in there I wouldn't have...

PAUL
I am glad that you have shot this
footage -- and that the world will
see it. It is the only way we have
a chance that people might
intervene.

Jack glances down.

JACK
Yeah, and if no one intervenes, is
it still a good thing to show?

PAUL
How can they not intervene -- when
they witness such atrocities?

JACK
(sighs) I think if people see this
footage, they'll say, "Oh my God,
that's horrible," and then go on
eating their dinners.

Paul looks shocked. Jack quickly realizes his lack of
sensitivity.

JACK (CONT'D)
What the hell do I know? Listen...
you wanna just relax...?

                    PAUL
          No. I have more work to do. Thank
          you for your offer. Please enjoy
          your evening, Mr. Daglish.

Paul walks off.

EXT. HOTEL MILLE COLLINES - GROUNDS - DAY

Sounds of gunfire. A stampede of Tutsi refugees come from
the gate, flee up the driveway.

Paul arrives, watches in horror as more refugees pour into
his hotel.

Dube finds Paul.

                    DUBE
          Sir, sir. We've got trouble at the
          gate.

                    REFUGEES
          Help! Please help us. Please,
          please.

EXT. HOTEL MILLE COLLINES - FRONT GATE - DAY

As Jack films, Paul arrives by the gate house. UN soldiers
watch the outside road. More refugees burst through the
gate. One of the last to make it is Benedict, dressed only
in boxer shorts, covered in blood from a large machete slash
in his head.

PANDEMONIUM.

                    1ST MALE REFUGEE
          They're after us!

                    2ND MALE REFUGEE
          Help!

                    3RD MALE REFUGEE
          Can we have some medical assistance
          here, please?

                    FEMALE REFUGEE
          Please help us, please, please.

Benedict stumbles toward Jack and Peter.

Paul grabs Benedict, tries to calm him as Colonel Oliver's
jeep roars in beside them.

> COLONEL OLIVER
> Right, fall back everybody...

> PAUL
> What is it? Please, what is
> happening?

> BENEDICT
> They're, they're killing everyone.
> The lady...

> COLONEL OLIVER (O.S.)
> The Interahamwe have surrounded the
> hotel, they're coming up the road.
> Come on.

He helps Benedict into a UN truck. It drives off to the
hotel.

Colonel Oliver orders his lieutenants to the roadside.

> COLONEL OLIVER (CONT'D)
> Cover the road. Now.

A convoy of pickup trucks pull up outside the gate. Drunken
Militia men on the back wave spears, machetes, one in a
woman's disco wig, waves a cordless power drill. The drill
bit is red with blood.

In the next truck, two Militia men triumphantly taunt the UN
soldiers as they hold blue UN helmets high on sticks. The
helmets are shot through with holes.

Enraged UN soldiers cock their weapons, aim.

> COLONEL OLIVER (CONT'D)
> Stand your ground. Do not shoot --
> Do not shoot!

The Colonel stabilizes the situation, his men watch as a
Militiaman throws a UN helmet, riddled with bullets, at their
feet.

The Militia drive away.

> COLONEL OLIVER (CONT'D)
> Lieutenant, guard this gate.

Colonel Oliver walks to Paul.

                         COLONEL OLIVER
            They murdered my men. I lost ten
            Belgian soldiers. They were
            protecting your lady Prime
            Minister.

                         PAUL
            She is dead?

                         COLONEL OLIVER
            Yeah, she's dead. The Europeans
            are putting together an
            intervention force. They'll be
            here in a few days.

                         PAUL
            Yes, I understand that, Colonel,
            but there is simply no place for me
            to put all these people.

                         COLONEL OLIVER
            Paul, Paul...what can I do? I'll
            put two more men on the gate, two
            of my best lieutenants.

                         PAUL
                  (reluctant)
            All right.

INT. HOTEL MILLE COLLINES - BAR - NIGHT

The Red Cross worker, Pat Harper, downs a large brandy in a
single gulp. Paul and Tatiana arrive.

                         PAUL
            Madame Archer.

                         PAT ARCHER
            Hello.

                         PAUL
            We were expecting you five days
            ago.

                         PAT ARCHER
            I'm sorry.

                         TATIANA
            My brother and his family, did, did
            you find them?

> PAT ARCHER
> I made it to the house but it was
> empty.

> TATIANA
> Empty?

> PAT ARCHER
> It had been ransacked. As I left,
> an old woman, she waved to me. I
> went to the house. She has the two
> little girls. They're safe.

> TATIANA
> But...my brother and his wife, did
> the old lady know of them?

Pat shakes her head NO. Tatiana holds back tears.

> TATIANA (CONT'D)
> My brother is dead. They would
> never leave their children.

> PAUL
> Perhaps they could not make it
> home, Tatiana. They are, they are
> in hiding. (TO PAT) Please, can
> you return and bring the girls back
> here to us?

> PAT ARCHER
> I, I can't. There are Interahamwe
> roadblocks everywhere.

Tatiana is devastated.

> PAT ARCHER (CONT'D)
> When I reached the orphanage, the
> Interahamwe were there. They'd
> already started killing children.
> They made me watch. There was one
> girl -- she had her little sister
> wrapped on her back.

Tears run down her face as she continues.

> PAT ARCHER (CONT'D)
> As they were about to chop her, she
> cried out to me. (UPSET) "Please
> don't let them kill me, I, I, I
> promise I won't be Tutsi anymore."

Tatiana can't take any more. She stands up to leave.

                         TATIANA
          Please, I -- I can't.

                         PAT ARCHER
          They're targeting Tutsi children to
          wipe out the next generation. I've
          nowhere to take the orphans, Paul.

                         PAUL
          Don't worry, there will be an
          intervention force coming soon.
          They will get the orphans out then.

EXT. HOTEL MILLE COLLINES - GROUNDS - DAY

Paul and Tatiana push through the French tourists and AID
workers running across the lobby.

                         FRENCH TOURISTS
          They're here.

French and Belgian special forces pull into the parking lot,
standing tall in their jeeps, macho western super troops,
triumphant. Salvation! Jack films.

Wild cheering, kisses. Westerners, Rwandans, dance and sing
in celebration.

Guests shake the soldiers' hands, kiss them.

                         4TH FEMALE GUEST
          Thank goodness.

Paul smiles with relief as he watches the jubilation.

Colonel Oliver passes Paul.

                         COLONEL OLIVER
          Well done.

Oliver walks to a group of the French soldiers.

                         COLONEL OLIVER
          About time, gentlemen.

Tatiana walks over, carrying Roger.

                         TATIANA
          It's okay, Roger, we're safe now.

Colonel Oliver is off to the side, with the commanders of the
French and Belgian officers. Paul watches but cannot hear.

> ODETTE (TO TATIANA)
> Jean Baptiste, our prayers have
> been answered.

> TATIANA
> See, it's okay.

Suddenly Oliver pulls off his blue beret, throws it on the ground, points his finger at the French and Belgian officers.

Oliver storms off, returns, picks up his beret.

Paul watches as he storms into the lobby.

Paul follows.

INT. HOTEL MILLE COLLINES - BAR - DAY

Paul follows the Colonel into the bar. The places is empty, the bartender missing, gone to celebrate. Colonel Oliver sits, dejected.

> PAUL
> So, Colonel, what can I get for
> you?

> COLONEL OLIVER
> Well...something strong.

> PAUL
> Scotch?

> COLONEL OLIVER
> Yeah.

Oliver cracks a weary smile. Paul pours two drinks, slides one across. He raises a glass.

> PAUL
> Congratulations, Colonel. You have
> performed a minor miracle.

> COLONEL OLIVER
> (raw cynicism)
> Congratulations, huh?

> PAUL
> Yes, sir.

> COLONEL OLIVER
> You should spit in my face.

                        PAUL
            Excuse me, Colonel?

                        COLONEL OLIVER
            You're dirt. We think you're dirt,
            Paul.

                        PAUL
            Who is we?

Oliver shakes his head.

                        COLONEL OLIVER
            The West, all the superpowers,
            everything you believe in, Paul.
            They think you're dirt. They think
            you're dumb. You're worthless.

                        PAUL
            I'm afraid I don't understand what
            you are saying, sir.

                        COLONEL OLIVER
            Oh, come on, don't bullshit me,
            Paul. You're the smartest man
            here. You got 'em all eating out
            of your hands. You could own this
            hotel, except for one thing.

Paul doesn't answer.

                        COLONEL OLIVER (CONT'D)
            You're black. You're not even a
            nigger, you're African! They're
            not gonna stay, Paul. They're not
            gonna stop the slaughter.

Oliver downs his drink and leaves.

INT. HOTEL MILLE COLLINES - PAUL'S ROOM - NIGHT

Paul opens the door. Tatiana and the kids play cards.

                        PAUL
            Hello.

                        ELYS
            Hello, daddy.

                        PAUL
            Elys, take Diane in the other room.

Elys stands and Diane moves to follow. Tatiana looks at
Paul, puzzled, as he sits beside her.

> TATIANA
> What is it?

> PAUL
> All the whites are leaving.
> They're being evacuated.

Tatiana's grip tightens.

> TATIANA
> What about us?

> PAUL
> We have been abandoned.

Tatiana clings to hope.

> TATIANA
> But the soldiers -- will stop the
> killers.

Paul loses it.

> PAUL
> Listen, listen to me. Tatsi,
> listen. I said all the whites are
> leaving. The French, the Italians,
> even the UN Belgian soldiers. All
> of them.

> TATIANA
> Who is left?

> PAUL
> I don't know. Colonel Oliver says
> he has three hundred UN
> peacekeepers for the whole country.
> The most he can spare for the hotel
> are four men.

He takes her hand, makes her sit down.

> PAUL (CONT'D)
> And they are not allowed to shoot.
> (a beat) I am a fool.

> TATIANA
> No.

                    PAUL
    They told me I was one of them and
    I...the wine, chocolates, cigars,
    style. I swallowed it. I
    swallowed it, I swallowed all of
    it. And they handed me their shit.
    I have no, no history -- I have no
    memory. I, I'm a fool, Tatsi.

                    TATIANA
    You are no fool. I know who you
    are.

She takes his hand.

EXT. HOTEL MILLE COLLINES - FORECOURT - DAY

It's raining. A chaos of luggage, white tourists, AID agency
people line up to leave.

On the edges, Rwandans, watching, silent, fearful.

French and Italian commanders check off names on clipboards.

                    NEWSREADER (V.O. - THRU RADIO)
    News service Africa. A United
    Nations source reports that the US
    and British representatives on the
    Security Council will lobby for the
    removal of all UN peacekeepers from
    Rwanda.

Paul watches as the final agency people are loaded on the
buses.

Several white AID workers weep uncontrollably as they are
dragged away from frightened Rwandan co-workers.

The young hooker Chloe begs Jack to take her with him, as a
soldier stops Peter the sound man because he is black.

                    CHLOE
    Please, Jack, please don't go.

                    JACK (TO SOLDIER)
    Wait, he's British.
            (TO PETER)
    Got your passport?

Peter takes his passport from his shirt pocket and hands it
to the soldier. Chloe clings to Jack, she's terrified.

                    CHLOE
         Jack, please don't leave me,
         please. Please, please!

Jack needs another minute with Chloe.

                    CHLOE
         Please don't leave me. Please,
         Jack. They'll put me on the
         street. They'll chop me.

He digs into his pockets, pulls out money, cigarettes, credit
cards. Everything he has, he gives to her.

                    JACK
         Here. Now, take this...take this.

                    CHLOE
         No, no, no, no, no...

                    JACK
         Just take the money. Please just
         take the money.

He tries to hand the money to her.

Paul is trying to usher the European aid workers onto the
buses.

                    PAUL
         You must go, you must. Please,
         they are waiting.

Jack sees Paul and waves him over.

                    JACK
         Paul!

                    PAUL
         They are waiting.

                    JACK
         Paul. He won't put you out,
         here...

Jack hands money and credit cards to Paul.

                    JACK (CONT'D)
         ...give her anything she wants.
         Anything. Just charge it.

                    PAUL
         This is not necessary.

Chloe clings to Jack.

                    JACK
          I can't...

He is deeply ashamed.

                    CHLOE
          They're gonna kill us here. Jack,
          take me with you.

Paul holds on to Chloe.

                    PAUL
          Let him go. We have to let him go.

A porter rushes toward Jack with an umbrella. Jack waves him
away.

                    JACK
          Oh, don't, don't do that please.

He looks at David. He can't believe that they're deserting
the Rwandan people and one is still trying to keep him dry.

                    JACK (CONT'D)
          I'm so ashamed.

Jack, Peter and David walk towards the bus, followed by
French and Belgian captains.

Suddenly there is a disturbance on the driveway.

                    NUN (O.S.)
          Wait!

                    PRIEST (O.S.)
          Hold the buses!

A group of French nuns, alongside Rwandan nuns, with maybe a
hundred Tutsi women and children come running up the
driveway. They are all terrified. One nun leads with a
French flag. The Belgian soldiers form a line stopping the
new refugees.

A Priest speaks with the Belgian Captain.

                    PRIEST
          Thank you for being here. Thank
          you very much.

The Belgian Captain shakes his head NO.

>   BELGIAN CAPTAIN
> No Rwandans.
>
>   PRIEST
> What?
>
>   BELGIAN CAPTAIN
> Foreign nationals only. Sorry,
> Father, those were the orders.
>
>   PRIEST
> But you can't leave the children
> behind.
>
>   BELGIAN CAPTAIN
> Sorry, Father, we have our orders.
>
>   PRIEST
> You can't leave them.
>
>   BELGIAN CAPTAIN
> We can do no more.

Soldiers begin pulling white nuns from the terrified crowd.

Several nuns begin hysterically weeping, pulling Rwandan nuns and children with them. Panic breaks out among the crowd.

Jack grabs his camera, pushes off the bus.

Paul pushes into the crowd as the rain pours down on them.

>   PAUL
> Father, it is of no use.
>
>   BELGIAN CAPTAIN
> Get these nuns on the bus.
>
>   PAUL
> These men are not here, they are
> not here to help us. Please there
> is nothing we can do. Get your
> people on the bus, I'll take care
> of my people.
>
>   PRIEST
> But -- we must take them with us.
>
>   PAUL
> It is of no use, Father. Please,
> hurry.

The white nuns are ushered onto the buses as the Rwandan nuns and refugees are pushed toward the hotel, away from the buses.

One nun tries to bring a boy with her onto the bus, but a soldier pulls them apart.

Paul takes the boy.

> PAUL
> Please go to the hotel.

Jack films, as a FRENCH OFFICER screams at him, a tug-of-war with the camera, Jack using it as a ram. David intervenes.

> DAVID
> Sir, please don't touch the camera.
> We have the right to film.

> SOLDIER
> No filming. No filming.

Children are crying all around them. Paul tries to usher them into the hotel.

> PAUL
> Go to the hotel. Go inside. Go
> inside the hotel. All of you. Yes
> you can stay. Yes, we will take
> care of you. Go into the hotel.

Paul looks to Colonel Oliver, who stands drenched, alone in the rain.

The convoy -- French jeeps, buses, Italian jeeps, UN jeeps -- takes off.

Paul stands in the rain, watching the buses leave. Dube pushes his way through the crowd. He opens an umbrella and hurries toward Paul.

> DUBE
> Sir.

Where five minutes before, the courtyard was a frenzy of wealthy Europeans and aid workers, the groups of clustered black faces are silent except for the crying of babies and sobbing mothers. Paul picks his way among them.

> PAUL
> Come. Please, everyone inside.
> Please, people, let's go inside.
> Out of the rain, please.

INT. HOTEL MILLE COLLINES - PAUL'S ROOM - NIGHT

Paul and Tatiana in bed in each other's arms, silent, abandoned.

>   TATIANA
>   Paul.

He turns to her.

>   TATIANA (CONT'D)
>   I want you to go. You take the
>   children. You go get the girls.
>   Your card says Hutu.

>   PAUL
>   (shocked)
>   What are you saying?

>   TATIANA
>   No, please, please. You pay money
>   at the roadblocks. I want you to
>   go.

>   PAUL
>   No, Tatiana, no. I will never
>   leave you. I will never leave you.
>   Shh. Oh Tatsi. Let us sleep, my
>   wife, let us sleep.

She breaks down and cries, he kisses her.

INT. HOTEL MILLE COLLINES - PAUL'S ROOM - DAY

Paul and Tatiana are in bed, asleep. A gun barrel appears, pushes against Paul's chest. A HUTU LIEUTENANT stands over Paul, holding the gun to his head. Other soldiers move through the room.

>   HUTU LIEUTENANT
>   Get up, get up.

>   HUTU LIEITENANT (CONT'D)
>   Are you the manager?

>   PAUL
>   Yes, sir. What, what's the matter?

>   HUTU LIEITENANT
>   Everyone must leave the hotel now.

                    PAUL
        Why?

                    ELYS (O.S.)
        Papa, what's wrong.

                    HUTU LIEUTENANT
        It's an order.

                    PAUL
        I need some time. Twenty, thirty
        minutes to take a shower. Sir,
        people are still sleeping.

The Lieutenant is not impressed.

                    HUTU LIEUTENANT
        I don't care.

                    PAUL
        Please, let me get you some beers
        for you and your boys. And I'll be
        down right away. As quick as I
        can.

"Cold beers" softens the soldiers' attitudes.

                    HUTU LIEUTENANT
        Ten minutes.

                    PAUL
        Yes, sir, ten minutes.

The soldiers march off. The kids clutch on to Tatiana.
Suddenly Tatiana notices Roger is missing.

                    TATIANA
        Roger's not here.

                    PAUL
        Where is he? Where's Roger?

Diane points.

                    DIANE
        Under the bed.

Paul kneels by the bed and looks underneath. He sees Roger
trembling under the bed.

                    PAUL
        Roger? Shh, shh, shh. It's papa.
        They've gone. They've gone.

He pulls Roger to him, slides him out, clutches him in his arms, then turns him over to Tatiana as he considers what to do next.

>   PAUL
> Go to the roof, Tatiana.

>   TATIANA
> The roof?

>   PAUL
> Yes, yes, go to the roof right now.

He hurries out.

INT. HOTEL MILLE COLLINES - MANAGER'S OFFICE - DAY

Paul sits by the phone and dials.

>   PAUL
> Yes, good day. General Bizimungu,
> please...

ANOTHER CALL

>   PAUL (CONT'D)
> He is where?

ANOTHER CALL

>   PAUL (CONT'D)
> No, that is unacceptable. Who
> would order such a th...

ANOTHER CALL

>   PAUL (CONT'D)
> Yes, did you find the General?

EXT. HOTEL MILLE COLLINES - ENTRANCE - DAY

Soldiers are everywhere. The Hutu Lieutenant waits in his jeep. Dube walks toward them with a tray of beers.

>   DUBE
> Gentlemen, please have some beers.

>   HUTU LIEUTENANT
> Get me the guest list.

                    DUBE
          Yes, sir.

Dube spills his beer in his haste and fear.

INT. SABENA OFFICES - BELGIUM - TILLEN'S OFFICE - DAY

The Sabena President and three VPs have an early morning
meeting. The intercom buzzes.

                    TILLENS
          Yes?

                         SECRETARY (V.O. - THRU SPEAKER PHONE)
                    Sorry, sir, but I have a call from
                    Paul in Kigali. He says it's
                    urgent.

The President hits the speaker button.

                    TILLENS
          Paul. Are you all right?

                         PAUL (V.O. - THRU SPEAKER PHONE)
                    We have a big problem, sir.

                    TILLENS
          What?

                         PAUL (V.O. - THRU SPEAKER PHONE)
                    The Hutu Army have come. They've
                    ordered us -- all of us -- out of
                    the hotel.

                    TILLENS
          Why are they doing this?

                         PAUL (V.O. - THRU SPEAKER PHONE)
                    I think they will kill us all.

                    TILLENS
               (stunned)
          Kill? What do you mean...all? How
          many?

                         PAUL (V.O. - THRU SPEAKER PHONE)
                    We have one hundred staff, and now
                    more than eight hundred guests.

Tillens can barely form words to reply.

                         TILLENS
          Eight hundred!

                         PAUL (V.O. - THRU SPEAKER PHONE)
          Yes, sir. There are now eight
          hundred Tutsi and Hutu refugees. I
          do not have much time left, sir. I
          want to thank you for everything
          you have done for me and my family,
          and please thank all of my friends
          at Sabena.

The President considers this.

                         TILLENS
          Paul, wait. I'm gonna put you on
          hold. Stay by the phone.

He hits the hold button, looks to the other executives. They
are stunned to silence by Paul's profound farewell.

INT. HOTEL MILLE COLLINES - MANAGER'S OFFICE - DAY

Paul sits in the office, his hand over the mouthpiece. From
the lobby come soldiers' angry voices.

                         SOLDIER (O.S.)
          Where are your papers?

INT. SABENA OFFICES - BELGIUM - TILLEN'S OFFICE - DAY

The President gets everyone working on the phone.

                         TILLENS
          Louis, get on to the UN. Tell them
          what's happening. Mary, call the
          Prime Minister's office. Tell them
          I must speak with him now.

The President lifts the telephone receiver and hits a button.

                         TILLENS
          Paul, are you there?

                         PAUL (V.O. - THRU SPEAKER PHONE)
          Yes, sir.

                         TILLENS
          Who can I call to stop this?

Paul thinks.

                    PAUL (V.O. - THRU SPEAKER PHONE)
          The French -- they supply the Hutu
          Army.

                    TILLENS
          Do everything you can to bide time.
          I'll call you right back.

Paul hurries from the room.

INT. HOTEL MILLE COLLINES - LOBBY - DAY

Dube is at the computer, printing something. Paul walks
quickly to him.

                    PAUL
          What are you doing, Dube?

                    DUBE
          The Lieutenant, sir. He wants to
          see the guest list.

Paul nervously glances at the soldiers.

                    PAUL
          Go and get these boys some more
          beer.

Dube walks to the bar to get the beer, and Paul is on the
computer, typing. A receptionist looks at the screen.

                    RECEPTIONIST
          Sir, that guest list is from two
          weeks ago.

                    PAUL
          Shh.

Paul hits the print button. The printer clicks to life.

INT. HOTEL MILLE COLLINES - ENTRANCE - DAY

Paul emerges with the printed registry. The Lieutenant
marches up to Paul.

                    HUTU LIEUTENANT
          Where's the guest list?

Paul hands him the print out. The Lieutenant studies it.

                    HUTU LIEUTENANT
Anderson, Arthurs, Boulier...What
is this?

                    PAUL
It is the guest list, sir.

                    HUTU LIEUTENANT
Are you trying to make a fool out
of me?

                    PAUL
No. We stopped taking names after
the President was murdered. This
is the only guest list, sir.

                    HUTU LIEUTENANT
There are no Europeans left. Get
me the names of all the cockroaches
in there, now.

                    PAUL
That will take time.

                    HUTU LIEUTENANT
You don't have time. If I don't
have the names so that I can pick
out the traitors, then I'll kill
everyone in there. Starting with
you.

The Lieutenant's radio comes to life and he turns to answer
it. He listens for a moment...

                    HUTU LIEUTENANT (INTO RADIO)
Yes, sir?

He angrily turns to Paul and grabs him.

                    HUTU LIEUTENANT
Who did you call?

                    PAUL
Who did I call?

                    HUTU LIEUTENANT
Don't lie to me! What is your
name?

                    PAUL
Rusesabagina. Paul Rusesabagina.

                         HUTU LIEUTENANT
            I'll remember you.

He prods Paul's chest.

                         HUTU LIEUTENANT (CONT'D)
            I'll remember you.

He turns to his soldiers, gestures.

                         HUTU LIEUTENANT (CONT'D)
            Let's go.

They drive off.

EXT. HOTEL MILLE COLLINES - ROOF - DAY

Paul emerges onto the roof. He looks around for his family,
sees Tatiana, his children and the neighbors sitting huddled
together.

                         PAUL
            They've gone.

                         TATIANA
            Oh.

Tatiana grabs him.

                         TATIANA (CONT'D)
            I was so afraid for you.

Dube appears.

                         DUBE
            Sir. The President of Sabena is on
            the phone for you.

Paul strokes Tatiana's face.

                         PAUL
            I must talk with this man.

INT. HOTEL MILLE COLLINES - MANAGER'S OFFICE - DAY

Paul hits the button and lifts the telephone receiver.

                         PAUL
            Mr. Tillens.

                    TILLENS (V.O. - THRU PHONE)
          Paul, what's going on?

Paul shakes his head in disbelief.

                    PAUL
          They left. Thank you, sir. What
          did you do?

INT. SABENA OFFICES - BELGIUM - TILLEN'S OFFICE - DAY

The Sabena President is at his desk.

                    TILLENS
          I got through to the French
          President's office.

                    PAUL (V.O. - THRU SPEAKER PHONE)
          Well, thank you. You have saved
          our lives.

                    TILLENS
          I pleaded with the French and the
          Belgians to go back and get you
          all. I'm afraid this is not going
          to happen.

Silence, Tillens is ashamed, angry.

                    TILLENS (CONT'D)
          They're cowards, Paul. Rwanda is
          not -- worth a single vote to any
          of them. The French, the British,
          the Americans. I am sorry, Paul.

INT. HOTEL MILLE COLLINES - MANAGER'S OFFICE - DAY

Paul is stunned.

                    PAUL
          Thank you.

INT. HOTEL MILLE COLLINES - FUNCTION ROOM - DAY

The refugees are gathered, Paul addresses them.

                    PAUL
          There will be no rescue. No
          intervention force. We can only
          save ourselves.
                              (MORE)

                    PAUL (cont'd)
          Many of you know influential people
          abroad. You must call these
          people.

INT. HOTEL MILLE COLLINES - MANAGER'S OFFICE - DAY

MONTAGE of influential refugees. Odette, Benedict, Xavier
call, plead, write and send faxes.

Odette sits at the desk, on the phone.

                    PAUL (V.O.)
          You must tell them what will happen
          to us.

Other refugees are on the phones.

                    PAUL (V.O. CONT'D)
          Say goodbye. But when you say
          goodbye, say it as though you are
          reaching through the phone and
          holding their hand. Let them know
          that if they let go of that hand...
          you will die. We must shame them
          into sending help. Most
          importantly, this can not be a
          refugee camp. The Interahamwe
          believe that the Mille Collines is
          a four-star Sabena hotel. That is
          the only thing keeping us alive.

INT. HOTEL MILLE COLLINES - LOBBY - DAY

Paul on the move, organizing, walks to the receptionist at
the front desk.

                    PAUL
          Have you printed the bills?

She hands him a stack of envelopes.

                    PAUL (CONT'D)
          Now please erase the registry.

                    RECEPTIONIST
          Erase it?

                    PAUL
          Yes. I want no names to appear
          there.

Dube joins him.

                         DUBE
          Boss, the carpenters are ready.

                         PAUL
          Tell them to remove all of the
          numbers from the doors.

                         DUBE
          And put what?

                         PAUL
          And put nothing.

INT. HOTEL MILLE COLLINES - HALLWAY - DAY

Paul goes door to door, knocking. The rooms are all packed
with Tutsi refugees. A door opens. He hands an envelope to
the refugee.

                         PAUL
          Good day. Here is your bill for
          the last week. If you cannot pay,
          or think you will not be able to
          pay, please go to the banquet room
          and Dube will take care of you.
          Thank you.

EXT. HOTEL MILLE COLLINES - GROUNDS - NIGHT

Refugees are clustered on the ground, in tents, as the radio
voice plays over a reporter's interview of a State Department
Officer.

                         AMERICAN REPORTER (V.O. - THRU RADIO)
          Does the State Department have a
          view as to whether or not what is
          happening -- could be genocide?

                         STATE DEPARTMENT OFFICER (V.O. - THRU
                         RADIO)
          We have every reason to believe
          that acts of genocide have
          occurred.

Inside his office Paul and the others listen.

                         BRITISH REPORTER (V.O. - THRU RADIO)
          How many acts of genocide does it
          take to make genocide?

> STATE DEPARTMENT OFFICER (V.O. - THRU
> RADIO)
> Alan, that's not a question that
> I'm in a position to answer.

> BRITISH REPORTER (V.O. - THRU RADIO)
> Is it true that you have specific
> guidance not to use the word
> genocide in isolation, but always
> to preface it with this word, "acts
> of"?

> STATE DEPARTMENT OFFICER (V.O. - THRU
> RADIO)
> I have guidance which I try to use
> as best I can. There are
> formulations that we are using that
> we are trying to be consistent in
> our use of.

Paul is listening to all of this. Benedict turns off the
radio in disgust.

INT. HOTEL MILLE COLLINES - BAR - DAY

General Bizimungu is at a table. Across the bar Gregoire and
his girlfriend laugh. Paul pours the General a drink.

> PAUL
> I'm sorry it is not Glenmorangie.

> GENERAL BIZIMUNGU
> As long as it is scotch.

He lifts the glass, drinks.

> GENERAL BIZIMUNGU (CONT'D)
> Your white friends have abandoned
> you.

> PAUL
> So it would seem.

> GENERAL BIZIMUNGU
> Well, don't worry. I will take
> care of you.

> PAUL
> I'm glad to hear that, because...
> I was wondering if perhaps you
> could spare us a few policemen? To
> protect us, sir.

                    GENERAL BIZIMUNGU
          The police are very busy, Paul.

                    PAUL
          Yes, I am aware of this, but when I
          last spoke to the President of
          Sabena, he assured me that anyone
          who helped protect Belgian property
          would be well rewarded.

Bizimungu considers this.

                    GENERAL BIZIMUNGU
          I will see what I can do.

                    PAUL
          Excuse me momentarily, sir.

INT. HOTEL MILLE COLLINES - STOREROOM - DAY

Paul fills Bizimungu's briefcase with scotch, hands two six-
packs of beer to Dube. Paul notes his once-packed storeroom
is now considerably dwindled in stock.

                    PAUL
          Where has all our beer gone?

                    DUBE
          Sir, Gregoire has been taking beer.

                    PAUL
          How much beer?

                    DUBE
          Many.

INT. HOTEL MILLE COLLINES - BAR - DAY

Paul arrives back at the bar, hands Bizimungu his briefcase.
Dube gives the beer to the soldiers.

Gregoire is still flirting with his girlfriend.

                    GREGOIRE
          And then he says to me, "How do you
          get the girls?"

He notices Paul with the General.

GREGOIRE (CONT'D)
There's our cockroach manager.
Always kissing ass.

Paul sits again with the General.

PAUL
...I'm glad you came by. I
overheard something that I think
you should know about.

GENERAL BIZIMUNGU
What did you overhear?

PAUL
It was a discussion between a UN
Colonel and an American Embassy
official.

GENERAL BIZIMUNGU
And what did they say?

PAUL
The American assured the Colonel
that they would watch everything.

GENERAL BIZIMUNGU
How? They're gone, Paul.

Paul points surreptitiously to the sky.

PAUL
With their spies. Satellites.

GENERAL BIZIMUNGU
(laughs)
Americans.

Gregoire's girlfriend giggles. Paul looks over at them.

PAUL
You know, I admire you, General.
How do you keep command of your men
amidst such madness?

GENERAL BIZIMUNGU
I am a strong man, Paul.

PAUL
I wish I were more like you. I
mean, look at my staff.

He motions to Gregoire and his girlfriend.

                    PAUL (CONT'D)
He won't work. Listens to no one.

                GENERAL BIZIMUNGU
He is staff?

                    PAUL
Oh yes.

Gregoire is engaged with his girlfriend and doesn't notice
the General approach. The General grabs the ice bucket and
sloshes the icy water over Gregoire.

                GENERAL BIZIMUNGU
Get back to work, you slug. Go!

The girlfriend and Gregoire flee.

INT. HOTEL MILLE COLLINES - PAUL'S ROOM - NIGHT

The kids are asleep on the floor all around the bed. Paul
and Tatiana are on the bed.

                    TATIANA
            (laughs)
Satellites?

                    PAUL
Well, what was I going to say?
That the Americans were hiding in
the trees?

Paul remembers something. A cloud of anxiety washes over
him.

                    TATIANA
What's the matter?

                    PAUL
I have to go out and get food.

                    TATIANA
            (alarmed)
Go out? Where?

                    PAUL
To George Rutagunda's place.

                    TATIANA
No!

                    PAUL
          I have to, Tatiana. We are only as
          valuable as the money we give to
          him.

                    TATIANA
          You cannot go alone.

                    PAUL
          I'm not going alone. I'll take
          Gregoire with me. He's a good
          Hutu. And he wants to impress me
          now.

INT. HOTEL MILLE COLLINES - LOBBY - NIGHT.

4 a.m. The lobby is deserted except for Gregoire in uniform
behind the front desk, lit by candlelight.

                    PAUL
          It is good to see you back at work,
          Gregoire.

Gregoire wakens quickly.

                    GREGOIRE
          Please, accept my humblest
          apologies...

                    PAUL
          We have a job this morning. We are
          going to see George Rutagunda.
          Please get the van.

EXT. KIGALI STREETS - NIGHT

The van passes along the deserted main road, past a line of
flaming houses.

EXT. GEORGE RUTAGANDA'S WAREHOUSE - NIGHT

The van pulls up by Rutagunda's warehouse. Now it is guarded
by two Interahamwe trucks and twenty drunken Militia.

                    MILITIAMAN
          Show me your ID.

Paul gets out, shows his ID. Paul walks through the gate as
RTLM radio plays.

                    RADIO PRESENTER (V.O. - THRU RADIO)
          Remember how those Tutsi women used
          to look down their long noses at
          Hutu men? Now they beg for their
          lives. I say taste those Tutsi
          whores before they die.

EXT. GEORGE RUTAGANDA'S WAREHOUSE - NIGHT

The courtyard is stacked with ammunition cases. In a far
corner there are a group of figures hidden inside a barbed
wire enclosure. Paul focuses on them in the half darkness,
realizes they are young women, most of them naked or in
shredded clothes. Systematic rape victims.

Three trucks roar up. George Rutagunda, heavily armed, in
cut-off shorts and an open shirt, his barrel chest laden with
bandoliers.

                    GEORGE
          Hey, Paul, my old friend.

As they approach the warehouse door, Paul can't help staring
at the women as they pass. Behind them a militiaman drags
and kicks a young Tutsi woman off a truck.

                    GEORGE (CONT'D)
          Tutsi prostitutes and witches. So --
          what can I do for you?

                    PAUL
          I need supplies, George.

                    GEORGE
          Any time, Paul. Any time.

INT. GEORGE RUTAGANDA'S WAREHOUSE - NIGHT

The warehouse is now filled with looted televisions, artwork,
cars. George points to the stacks of beer.

                    GEORGE
          Paul, everything is double the
          price now. You understand that?

                    PAUL
          Yes. I need rice, beans, powdered
          milk, beer and your best whiskey.

                    GEORGE
          Beer, yes, but no whiskey.

                        PAUL
            You have no whiskey?

                        GEORGE
            No whiskey, no spirits. Your rich
            guests will have to do without
            their scotch. Anyway, Paul, I have
            bled that cow enough.

Paul counts out the Rwandan francs.

                        PAUL
            What are you saying, Geroge?

                        GEORGE
            Your rich cockroaches at the
            hotel...their money is no good to
            them any more. Soon, all the
            Tutsis will be dead.

                        PAUL (SHOCKED)
            You do not honestly believe that
            you can kill them all?

                        GEORGE
            And why not? Why not? We are
            halfway there already.

Paul cannot believe what he is hearing. George walks away.

                        GEORGE (CONT'D)
            So, Paul, you want twelve bags of
            rice, eh?

He turns to a worker.

                        GEORGE (CONT'D)
            Give him twelve bags of rice and
            four crates of beer.

                        WORKER
            Yes, sir, right away.

                        GEORGE
            Oh, and Paul, I'll give you a crate
            of soft drinks for the kids. Free
            of charge.

                        PAUL
            Yes.

He turns back to Paul, walks with him to the van.

> GEORGE
> Let me give you a little tip, my
> friend. Our Generals in the Army
> say, "Don't go near the Mille
> Collines or they will send the
> Belgian soldiers back here." But
> soon, those Generals will have
> gone, and we will be in charge.
> It's time to butcher that fat cow
> of yours for the meat.

Paul gets into the van. George leans by the window.

> GEORGE (CONT'D)
> Maybe you could help us, Paul. You
> have some very important traitors
> at that hotel. Now, if we were to
> get them then maybe we will let you
> have one or two cockroaches of your
> own. Do you understand?

Paul says nothing, but Gregoire has been listening very
carefully.

> PAUL
> It is almost Dawn, George. We
> really must be going.

> GEORGE
> Take the river road back -- it's
> clear.

He smiles and taps the van door. The van takes off.

EXT. RIVER ROAD - DAWN

The van drives through the morning gray. Gregoire drives
fast, they drive into a bank of fog among trees. It is so
thick they can't see the road.

The van begins to bump erratically. Bump, bump, bump.

> PAUL
> Gregoire!

> GREGOIRE
> What is going on now?

> PAUL
> You've driven off the road.

              GREGOIRE
I'm on the road.

              PAUL
Stop, you're going to put us in the
river! Stop the car, stop the car!

The van jerks to a halt.

Paul clambers out, stumbles, falls.

And discovers he's looking at the face of a dead child, a
young Tutsi girl, he hands clasped on her ears as though to
block the sound of her own death -- an African Munz's scream.

Paul clambers to his feet, sees that the van is on a road
littered with dead bodies -- men, women, children.

The bumps were dead bodies, the van has driven over them.

A breeze from the river blows the fog clear for thirty feet.

REVEALING a carpet of bodies, hundreds of them sprawled all
along the road as far as Paul can see. Paul wanders around
misshapen corpses, made more ghostly by wisps of fog. Dogs
wander among the bodies, feeding. Vultures wait in trees.

Finally, Paul climbs shell-shocked back into the van.

Gregoire moves to start the van.

            PAUL (CONT'D)
Listen to me. You will tell no one
what you have seen here today. No
one, Gregoire.

Gregoire throws the van in reverse. They bump back over the
carpet of bodies, each shake and crunch another horror.

INT. HOTEL MILLE COLLINES - LOBBY - DAY

Paul enters a hallway, sees Dube.

              PAUL
Oh, Dube. Please help Gregoire to
unload the van.

Dube is puzzled by Paul's nervous haste.

INT. HOTEL MILLE COLLINES - MEN'S CHANGING ROOM - DAY

Paul steps into the room and closes the door. He looks at
his shirt cuff, now covered in blood. He takes a towel and
shirt from his locker, wipes his face, takes off his shirt.
He puts on a fresh shirt and tie, then looks down at his
wrongly fastened tie, laughs, then struggles to re-tie it.

Slowly he loses it. All of his stress of the past weeks
comes out. He rips off his shirt and leans against the wall,
slides to the floor, sobbing uncontrollably.

A knock at the door.

                    DUBE (O.S.)
          Sir? Sir, are you okay?

                    PAUL
          Don't come in.

                    DUBE (O.S.)
          Sir, are you okay?

                    PAUL
          Yes, I'm all right Dube. Don't
          come in, I'll be out...

Paul crawls on the floor, sobbing.

EXT. HOTEL MILLE COLLINES - GARDEN/SWIMMING POOL - DAY

Paul sits with Dube, as young girls practice dancing.

                    PAUL
          Hundreds. It was too many to
          count.

                    DUBE
          Why are people so cruel?

                    PAUL
          Hatred. Insanity. I don't know.

EXT. HOTEL MILLE COLLINES - GARDEN/SWIMMING POOL - NIGHT

Tatiana and Odette are feeding the children. Paul arrives
and steps to Tatiana, taking her arm.

                    TATIANA
          Hello.

                        PAUL
          Come with me.

                        TATIANA
          Where are we going?

                        PAUL
          Just come.

They slip out.

EXT. HOTEL MILLE COLLINES - ROOF - NIGHT.

Tatiana and Paul walk onto the roof. Artillery and mortar
fire rumble in the distance. Flashes silhouette along the
far hills above Kigali.

He leads her to a couch, a candle, two glasses and bottles of
beer. He pours a beer. They sit.

                        PAUL
          You like it?

                        TATIANA
          It is lovely. I hear we must pay
          for everything.

                        PAUL
          Yes, this is true.

                        TATIANA
          How much for this?

                        PAUL
          A kiss.

They kiss.

                        TATIANA
          You are a good man, Paul
          Rusesabagina.

                        PAUL
          I have a confession. When you
          worked as a nurse...

                        TATIANA
          In Ruhengeri?

                        PAUL
          Yes. When we first met. I had you
          transferred to Kigali.

                    TATIANA
What?

                    PAUL
I bribed the Minister of Health to
have you transferred to Kigali.

                    TATIANA
Why?

                    PAUL
To be closer. So I could marry
you.

                    TATIANA
What am I worth to you?

                    PAUL
It was substantial.

                    TATIANA
Tell me what it was.

                    PAUL
A car.

                    TATIANA
What sort of car?

                    PAUL
What does it matter?

                    TATIANA
I want to know.

                    PAUL
A Volkswagen.

                    TATIANA
        (laughs)
A Volks...I hope it was a new one!

She kisses him, total love. They lie back on the couch.

                    PAUL
We've had a good life, you and I.
I thank God every day -- for the
time we've had. (a beat) We have
to have a plan.

                    TATIANA
A plan?

                        PAUL
            Our children cannot see us die
            first. If the Militia come, you
            must come up here as quick as you
            can.

                        TATIANA
            Please, I don't want to...

She puts her hands to her ears. He pulls them down.

                        PAUL
            You must come up here, Tatiana.

                        TATIANA
            I don't want you to talk like this,
            please.

                        PAUL
            We have to, Tatiana. If I do not
            make it...you must take all of our
            children by the hand and you must
            jump.

                        TATIANA
            What are you saying? I could
            never...

                        PAUL
            You have to promise me. Tatiana.

She cries harder and squeezes his hand in fear.

                        TATIANA
            No, no, you don't...why, why are
            you saying...?

                        PAUL
            Tatiana, the machete is no way to
            die. You have to promise me you
            will do it.

                        TATIANA
            I cannot do...

                        PAUL
            You have to promise me, Tatiana.
            Please. Promise me you will do it.
            Please, Tatiana.

She looks at him. Finally amid the tears she nods yes.

He hugs her to him and places his hand on her head.

                    PAUL (CONT'D)
         Yes. I love you. I love you.

EXT. HOTEL MILLE COLLINES - ENTRANCE - DAY

Paul instructs the porters to clean around the entrance.
Diane, Elys, other kids run around, playing.

Paul appears.

The girls stop in front of him.

                    PAUL (CONT'D)
         Diane, Elys, now you know better.
         No one can be at the front of the
         hotel, I have told you this.

He turns to Dube.

                    PAUL (CONT'D)
         Take these children in the back.

The UN jeep comes up the driveway. Colonel Oliver gets out,
he waves a paper at Paul.

                    COLONEL OLIVER
         Paul. I've got good news.

INT. HOTEL MILLE COLLINES - FUNCTION ROOM - DAY

Oliver is on the stage, all the refugee guests, expectant,
are crowded into the room. He has a list in his hand.

                    COLONEL OLIVER
         Congratulations, your calls have
         worked. I have exit visas for the
         following families.

He reads.

                    COLONEL OLIVER (CONT'D)
         Bidori -- Kenya. Gituaranga --
         Zambia. Khalesa -- Belgium.

Elation among the chosen families.

Fear on the faces of the families who realize they have
missed this alphabetical list, anxiety among the others.

> COLONEL OLIVER (CONT'D)
> Dakuzi -- Kenya. Masambo --
> Zambia. Zinguru -- Ghana.
> Rusesabagina -- Belgium.

He hands the paper to Paul. Tatiana tries to comfort Odette, who has not been chosen.

> COLONEL OLIVER (CONT'D)
> All right, that's it. So remember,
> families be ready at 7 am.

Oliver jumps from the stage, pushes through the crowd to some UN soldiers, as Paul follows.

> PAUL
> Colonel. Surely Odette and Jean
> Baptiste are on the list?

Oliver shakes his head no.

> COLONEL OLIVER
> I'm sorry Jean, Odette. But I've
> been assured there will be another
> plane soon. Excuse me.

He moves off toward his men.

> ODETTE
> Don't worry, Tatsi, we'll make it
> to the next list.

The others leave. Tatiana is devastated.

> TATIANA
> The girls, Paul, I will not leave
> without them!

EXT. HOTEL MILLE COLLINES - FORECOURT - DAY

Pat hands over medical supplies from her Red Cross van. She hands a box to Paul.

> PAUL
> What have you brought us?

> PAT ARCHER
> Antibiotics, medical supplies.
> General first aid.

> PAUL
> Thank you.

                    PAT ARCHER
          I hear there's to be a convoy?

                    PAUL
          Yes.

                    PAT ARCHER
          Are you on the list?

Paul nods, almost embarrassed.

                    PAUL
          Madame Archer, I have an impossible
          request of you. Is there any way
          that you could return to the old
          woman and bring the girls back here
          to us?

                    PAT ARCHER
          Paul, that side of town has been
          destroyed in the fighting. They're
          probably dead.

                    PAUL
          Madame Archer, I'm begging you.
          Those girls have no one now.

He takes her hands, she relents.

                    PAT ARCHER
          I'll try.

                    PAUL
          We have to leave by 7 a.m.

                    PAT ARCHER
          Who'll take care of my orphans when
          you're gone?

                    PAUL
          Odette will care for them until we
          can get them out of here.

                    PAT ARCHER
          Tell me, Paul, what country's gonna
          take twenty Rwandan orphans?

                    PAUL
          I will find someone. I promise
          you.

                    PAT ARCHER
          Thanks.

HOTEL RWANDA

95.

PAUL
                    Thank you.

INT. HOTEL MILLE COLLINES - LOBBY - DAY

It's early next morning. The lucky families are gathered:
Tatiana and all her children, Xavier and his wife, Benedict,
others.

UN soldiers are helping the evacuees into the trucks.

                              RADIO   PRESENTER (V.O. - THRU RADIO)
                    Today a Red Cross representative
                    claimed that the death rate in the
                    Rwandan conflict may have climbed
                    to as many as five hundred thousand
                    victims. One report stated that
                    forty thousand bodies had been
                    removed from Lake Victoria.

Odette, Tatiana and the children are waiting outside as Paul
paces, looking for Pat.

                         TATIANA
                    Where is she?

                         PAUL
                    I don't know. We wait until seven.
                    If she is not back with the girls
                    by then, she...she may not be
                    coming.

INT. HOTEL MILLE COLLINES - LOBBY - DAY

Paul herds the convoy people toward the door. A TUTSI MAN
hands Paul some letters.

                         MAN
                    Please, take these letters.

                         PAUL
                    Yes, I will take your letters.

Paul reaches out for the letters, takes them.

Other TUTSI REFUGEES hand letters to him and shake his hand.

                         PAUL
                    Yes, I am sorry.

                    2ND WOMAN
          Thank you. Thank you very much.

                    PAUL
          I am sorry. I wish I could have
          done more. I am sorry.

                    COLONEL OLIVER (O.S.)
          Keep moving. Keep moving. No, no,
          go round the back.

Paul embraces an old woman.

                    PAUL
          God be with you.

Paul's at a loss. He has to tear himself away.

Oliver and the UN soldiers check exit papers.

Afraid to look back, Paul heads for the convoy.

EXT. HOTEL MILLE COLLINES - ENTRANCE - DAY

The last of the evacuees clamber onto the UN trucks. The
children are waiting to board with Tatiana. Paul ushers them
onto the trucks.

                    PAUL
          Come. Come, children. Tatsi,
          come.

                    TATIANA
          Please, Paul, the girls. We wait a
          little while longer, please!

He shakes his head NO.

                    PAUL
          We cannot wait, Tatsi.

A UN soldier lifts Diane onto the truck.

                    UN SOLDIER
          Let's move out.

He gestures to the other soldiers to move out. Tatiana
climbs onto the truck and sits next to Benedict. Paul takes
Benedict's hand, moves to climb in truck.

                    FEMALE HOTEL WORKER
          Good luck, sir.

He looks back at the hotel. The unlucky refugees are now
crowded at the windows, lost souls watching out from their
prison at the lucky ones leaving.

The truck starts. Paul climbs onto the tailgate. He leans
into Benedict, whispers.

> PAUL
> I am not leaving. You hold
> Tatiana. Take care of my family.

Paul hops off the truck. Tatiana sees this, tries to follow.
Benedict grabs her.

> TATIANA
> Paul. Paul.

> PAUL
> I cannot leave these people to die.
> I cannot leave these people, Tatsi.

Tatiana and the children are wild with grief and fear.

> ROGER
> Papa!

> TATIANA
> No, no, no! Paul!

> ROGER
> Papa!

> PAUL
> Roger -- Roger, I will follow on
> the next flight.

He releases the tailgate and the truck drives away.

> TATIANA
> (screams)
> No, don't leave me!! Paul!!

> ROGER
> Papa!

> BENEDICT
> Don't worry. Don't worry,
> children, your father's going to be
> okay.

> ROGER
> I want Papa!

The convoy takes off down the driveway. Paul watches, then turns, walks downhearted across the lobby.

Gregoire watches him carefully.

INT. UN TRUCK - DAY

Tatiana comforts Roger.

> TATIANA
> Darling, it's okay --

> ROGER
> I want Papa!

> TATIANA
> It's okay it's...

INT. UN JEEP - DAY

Colonel Oliver sits next to a UN PAKISTANI DRIVER.

The convoy passes looters and small groups of Militia on the road but proceeds unheeded.

INT. HOTEL MILLE COLLINES - PAUL'S ROOM - DAY

The room is still littered with clothes, kids drawings, the personal junk accumulated over four weeks.

Paul tries to arrange things, then collapses on the couch, paralyzed with doubt -- why did he do this?

INT. HOTEL MILLE COLLINES - LOBBY - DAY

Dube, receptionists, porters are standing around the reception desk, listening to a radio.

> RADIO PRESENTER (V.O. - THRU RADIO)
> I say those Hutus who shelter the
> cockroaches are the same as
> cockroaches. They are all the
> same. Their fate should be the
> same.

EXT. HOTEL MILLE COLLINES - FORECOURT - DAY

Gregoire gets into the hotel van, drives off.

INT. HOTEL MILLE COLLINES - LOBBY - DAY

Dube, still listening to the radio, sees Gregoire leave in
the van.

EXT. UN TRUCK - DAY

The convoy continues toward the airport.

                        RADIO PRESENTER (V.O. - THRU RADIO)
                This is RTLM. We must fill the
                graves, good Hutus.

                        COLONEL OLIVER
                That goddamn radio station.

He glances at the driver.

EXT. ANOTHER KIGALI STREET - DAY

Gregoire is seated in the van, talking with an Interahamwe
man at a roadblock.

                        GREGOIRE
                Yeah, they are going to the
                airport.

The Interahamwe man raises a walkie-talkie.

EXT. UN TRUCK - DAY

The convoy continues on.

                        RADIO PRESENTER (V.O. - THRU RADIO)
                Stand by your radios. I am hearing
                some urgent news.

INT. HOTEL MILLE COLLINES - PAUL'S ROOM - DAY

There's a bang at the door.

                        DUBE
                Boss, please, come quick.

                        PAUL
                Not now, Dube.

> DUBE
> It is important. It is on the
> radio. You have to hear it.

He turns on the radio.

> RADIO PRESENTER (V.O. - THRU RADIO)
> ...this latest news, brothers. We
> have received reports of very
> important cockroaches and traitors
> trying to escape from the Mille
> Collines Hotel. Gather your
> weapons, stand by your radios, we
> will keep you informed. They are
> being smuggled away by United
> Nations....

> PAUL
> (stunned)
> No, no! Who told them of this,
> Dube?

> DUBE
> I saw Gregoire, sir. It is
> Gregoire. I saw him leaving in our
> bus.

EXT. KIGALI STREET - DAY

The convoy turns a bend. The streets are crowded with
Interahamwe men, dancing, singing war songs.

INT. HOTEL MILLE COLLINES - MANAGER'S OFFICE - DAY

Paul is on the phone, begging.

> PAUL
> Please, sir, I will give you
> everything I have.

> GENERAL BIZIMUNGU (ON PHONE)
> I say who leaves the hotel, and no
> one else.

> PAUL
> General Bizimungu, they are driving
> into an ambush!

EXT. KIGALI STREET - DAY

As the UN jeep turns a bend, Colonel Oliver SEES crowds of
Interahamwe swarming from beside houses, from gardens. They
pull burning tires, old furniture, junk into the road.

Interahamwe men run towards the convoy, clutching machetes.
Others overturn a burnt-out car on the road in front of the
UN trucks.

Oliver taps the driver's shoulder.

                    COLONEL OLIVER
          Slow down. Stay calm.

INT. UN TRUCK - DAY

The UN truck suddenly lurches, then slows. The refugees from
the Mille Collines grow alarmed.

                    MALE REFUGEE
          What is happening?

                    1ST FEMALE REFUGEE
          Oh my God, we're stopping.

                    2ND FEMALE REFUGEE
          We've stopped.

EXT. KIGALI STREET - DAY

Swarms of crazed Militia fill the road. A militiaman
approaches the truck.

                    INTERAHAMWE MAN
          You have got cockroaches in these
          trucks.

                    COLONEL OLIVER
          No, no. I've got UN personnel in
          these trucks. I've got permission
          to go through these roadblocks.

                    INTERAHAMWE MAN
          I'm going to search these trucks.

                    COLONEL OLIVER
          You are not going to search this
          convoy!

He looks in the sideview mirror and sees the Interahamwe climbing onto the trucks.

                    INTERAHAMWE MAN
          I am!

Oliver looks to the UN soldiers in his jeep.

                    COLONEL OLIVER
          Cover me!

He raises his gun and climbs out of the truck.

Militia men swarm around him as he pushes past to the truck. They smash the windshield and slash the canvas tarp with machetes.

Others move to the back and open the tailgate.

INT. UN TRUCK - DAY

Tatiana stands, moves the children to a corner of the truck, kicking at the hands that grab for her.

                    TATIANA
          Go to the back, go to the back!

                    ELYS
          Mama, please, what's happening,
          Mama?

The Interahamwe men jump into the truck.

Benedict is hauled from the truck. Beaten. Xavier is pulled from the truck, falls to the ground.

Oliver rushes over.

                    COLONEL OLIVER
          Get away from that truck. Get away
          from that truck. Now.

He pushes Interahamwe away from the truck, fights his way to Xavier and Benedict, fires warning shots into the ground.

                    COLONEL OLIVER (CONT'D)
          Get back. You're not to hurt these
          people.

                    UN SOLDIER
          Get back. Move back.

                    INTERAHAMWE MAN
          Look, I told you. You've got
          cockroaches in your truck.

                    COLONEL OLIVER
          No, no, no, they're political
          refugees under UN sanction.

EXT. HOTEL MILLE COLLINES - LOBBY - DAY

Paul and the others are still listening to the radio. They
can hear gunfire in the distance.

                    RADIO PRESENTER (V.O. - THRU RADIO)
          News has come to us that we have
          cowards in our own Army who will
          not let us punish them.

EXT. KIGALI STREET - DAY

The UN convoy is under attack by the Interahamwe. The
militiamen are waving machetes.

THEN HORNS -- RWANDAN SOLDIERS push between the Militia and
Colonel Oliver.

                    RWANDAN CAPTAIN
          You're moving cockroaches from
          Mille Collines?

                    COLONEL OLIVER
          No, sir. No, sir, they're
          political refugees.

                    RWANDAN CAPTAIN
          They cannot leave the Mille
          Collines.

An INTERAHAMWE MAN steps by.

                    INTERAHAMWE MAN
          They are not leaving!

He fires his gun at the truck tire. A Hutu soldier tries to
stop him.

                    RWANDAN CAPTAIN
          Stop him!

The Militia gunman fires wildly, wounds a RWANDAN SOLDIER in
the stomach.

                    RWANDAN CAPTAIN (CONT'D)
          You bastard!

The Rwandan Captain fires his gun into the air, his soldiers
begin to beat the Militia.

INT. UN TRUCK - DAY

Tatiana hides in the back, sheltering the children.   An
Interahamwe man points at her with his machete.

                    INTERAHAMWE MAN
          What's your name?

                    TATIANA
          I can't, I can't think...

EXT. KIGALI STREET - DAY

As the Hutu soldiers try to disperse the Militia, Colonel
Oliver shouts to his men.

                    COLONEL OLIVER
          Get everybody out of here. Move!
          Move it!

INT. UN TRUCK - DAY

The Interahamwe man threatens Tatiana.

                    INTERAHAMWE MAN
          What's your name? What's your
          name?

                    TATIANA
                  (terrified)
          Rusesabagina.

                    INTERAHAMWE MAN
          I said what's your name?

EXT. KIGALI STREET - DAY

Oliver yells to a soldier.

                    COLONEL OLIVER
          Let's move.

Benedict and Xavier climb into the back of the truck as it
starts to move. Oliver is right behind them. He sees the
Interahamwe man over Tatiana, points his gun at the thug.

>   COLONEL OLIVER
>   Get out! Get out or I'll shoot.

The man jumps out of the truck. The other Interahamwe jump
from the truck.

The trucks roar off -- back to the Mille Collines.

INT. HOTEL MILLE COLLINES - LOBBY - DAY

Paul, Dube and the others are listening to the radio.

>   RADIO PRESENTER (V.O. - THRU RADIO)
>   I am receiving more news, good
>   Hutus. I have learnt that the
>   traitor Rusesabagina's cockroaches
>   are on a truck. Ten thousand
>   francs for their heads!

Paul runs to a van, drives off.

INT. UN TRUCK - DAY

Colonel Oliver is helping, holding a towel around one wounded
refugee's neck. Tatiana is helping other wounded refugees.

>   OLIVER
>   Stay still. Stay still. Give me
>   your shirt, quickly.

EXT. HOTEL MILLE COLLINES - ENTRANCE - DAY

A LOUD ROAR as a UN truck, its tire shot out, screams up into
the forecourt. Paul almost collides with them. He races
after the truck, clambers in.

The convoy pulls up in front of the hotel. Bloody and
battered, the terrified refugees fall from the trucks.

Paul and Odette run among the casualties.

Paul helps refugees from the truck. Bloody refugees fill the
forecourt.

The other hotel staff help the wounded refugees.

Finally, Paul sees Tatiana.

> PAUL
> Oh, Tatiana, my darling. I was so
> worried about you. Tatiana.

He walks her toward the hotel entrance.

> PAUL (CONT'D)
> Tatiana! I was so worried.

> TATIANA
> You left me. You left me.

She runs off, joins the children. Paul tries to embrace her.
She REMOVES HER WEDDING RING, hands it to him.

> TATIANA
> Take this. I don't want it. I
> don't want it. You said you'd
> never leave me and you left me.

> PAUL
> I am so sorry. I am sorry.

> TATIANA
> You are a liar!

He embraces her, calms her down. She breaks into tears.

> COLONEL OLIVER (O.S.)
> Over here, over here.

> PAUL
> I'm sorry, I'm sorry, I'm sorry.

He takes the children's hands, tries to comfort them.

EXT. HOTEL MILLE COLLINES - GARDEN/SWIMMING POOL - DAY

Paul and his Tatiana walk by the pool.

> PAUL
> (apologizes)
> I wanted you to be safe.

> TATIANA
> That was not your decision to make.
> We make our decisions together.
> That was our promise.

                    PAUL
        You are right. You are right. I
        knew that the minute the truck
        pulled away. I'm sorry.

He looks toward the pool, where he sees Dube and the chefs
dipping cooking pots into the pool.

                    DUBE (O.S.)
        Come on, put some more water.

                    PAUL
        What are they doing?

Paul walks over, confused.

                    PAUL
        Dube?

                    DUBE
        I'm sorry, sir. They shut down the
        water. This is all we have.

EXT. HOTEL MILLE COLLINES - ENTRANCE - DAY

Bizimungu sits in his jeep. Paul arrives.

                    PAUL
        General, good day.

                    GENERAL BIZIMUNGU
        Where are my supplies?

                    PAUL
        I'm sorry, sir, the cellar is
        empty.

                    GENERAL BIZIMUNGU
        You have nothing -- and yet you
        call me begging for help? Do you
        know the trouble I have protecting
        these cockroaches?

Paul pulls a bundle of banknotes, hands them to the General.

                    PAUL
        Sir, I have money from the guests.

He snatches them from Paul, throws them to the ground, angry.

> GENERAL BIZIMUNGU
> Rwandan francs! Those are only
> good for wiping your ass. There is
> nothing more I can do for you,
> Paul. No more police, no more
> protection. Let the -- UN take
> care of you.

He looks away to his driver.

> GENERAL BIZIMUNGU (CONT'D)
> Drive. Go.

EXT. HOTEL MILLE COLLINES - GARDEN/SWIMMING POOL - DAY

Paul and Tatiana watch the clusters of families around their cooking fires. The pool is now half full.

> TATIANA
> (jokes)
> What would Sabena make of this?

Paul notices something by the fence. Then a flash. BANG!
He throws Tatiana to the ground, covers her.

> PAUL
> Watch out!

The rocket crashes through a hotel window and explodes.
Smoke and concrete dust fall around them. Refugees
screaming.

INT. HOTEL MILLE COLLINES - HALLWAY - DAY

Paul races along a smoke filled corridor. There is panic among the many frightened refugees. Paul finds Odette tending to a wounded woman.

> PAUL
> Are you hurt? Are you hurt? Go
> outside.

> ODETTE
> Please, stay still. There's glass
> here. I will get it out.

> PAUL
> Is anyone hurt, Odette?

> ODETTE
> Lots of cuts and bruises.

They discover the damaged room. It is a storeroom, covered
in burned linens and towels. Jean Baptiste works a fire
extinguisher.

                    PAUL
        Oh -- thank God it was a storeroom.

EXT. HOTEL MILLE COLLINES - GARDEN/SWIMMING POOL - DAY

Refugees camp out, huddled together. Women scoop water from
the pool. A group of refugees sit beneath a plastic sheet,
listening to a radio.

                    RADIO PRESENTER (V.O. - THRU RADIO)
        And in Rwanda, humanitarian
        agencies report that a rapid
        advance by the Tutsi rebel army has
        sparked a mass evacuation of Hutu
        refugees toward the Congo. One aid
        worker described it as the largest
        refugee exodus in modern history.

Colonel Oliver addresses a group of refugees.

                    COLONEL OLIVER
        The rebels have taken half the
        city, and they have proposed a deal
        the Hutu Generals are willing to
        accept. The rebels will exchange
        their Hutu prisoners...And you
        people, all of you, will be able to
        move behind rebel lines where it's
        safe.

Many are overjoyed but Tatiana is worried.

                    TATIANA
        The Interahamwe. What about them?

                    COLONEL OLIVER
        No one controls them.

                    BENEDICT
        This time they will kill us all.

                    PAUL
            (argues)
        They will kill us all if we stay
        here. We have to take the chance.
        What time should we be ready to
        leave?

>   COLONEL OLIVER
>   I can put it together in two days,
>   Paul.

>   ODETTE
>   Two days?

>   PAUL
>   Colonel, there is no way that we
>   can hold out for two days. I have
>   nothing left to bribe them with.
>   We will all be dead in two days.

Colonel Oliver is left alone, powerless to answer.

INT. HOTEL MILLE COLLINES - HALLWAY - NIGHT

Refugees sleep in the corridors.

INT. HOTEL MILLE COLLINES - PAUL'S ROOM - NIGHT

Diane sleeps between Paul and Tatiana. They all sleep
fitfully. He turns, looks at his wife and daughter. Diane
plays with a small cross on Tatiana's neck.

>   PAUL
>   (whispers)
>   Diane, shh, shh. Let your mother
>   rest. Go to sleep.

He looks at Tatiana's cross, then remembers.

>   PAUL (CONT'D)
>   Diplomat!

>   TATIANA
>   What?

>   PAUL
>   I have to go to the Diplomat!

EXT. HOTEL MILLE COLLINES - FORECOURT - DAY

Bizimungu's jeep arrives at the hotel. Paul greets him,
jumps in the back of the jeep.

>   GENERAL BIZIMUNGU
>   What are you doing?

                         PAUL
            We have to go to the Diplomat.

                   GENERAL BIZIMUNGU
            To do what?

                         PAUL
            Your items, they are there. Can
            you please put some policemen at
            the gate?

                   GENERAL BIZIMUNGU
            No. Let us see what you have to
            offer first.

INT. BIZIMUNGU'S JEEP - TRAVELLING - DAY

The jeep travels at high speeds along the road. Then the
driver sounds his horn -- a large crowd of Militia is
marching along the road, waving machetes and sticks.

Then he sees Pat's Red Cross van lying in a ditch, shot up
and trashed. He stares at it.

                         PAUL
            Oh, no. Madame Archer.

EXT. HOTEL DIPLOMAT - FORECOURT - DAY

The forecourt of the Diplomat has been turned into a mortar
position for the Hutu Army. They fire toward the Tutsi rebel
lines. The Hutu soldiers pack to leave the Diplomat. A
rebel mortar hits the forecourt, explodes.

The jeep pulls up to the door.

Paul and Bizimungu get out of the jeep. They run inside,
past a dying soldier.

INT. HOTEL DIPLOMAT - MANAGER'S OFFICE - DAY

Paul enters the manager's office, followed by the General.
He pulls back the bookshelf to reveal the safe. Opens the
safe door. CLICK.

He pulls it open, sees six bottles of Glenfiddich, four
bottles of VSOP brandy.

Paul takes a gold cross from the safe, hands it to Bizimungu.

                    PAUL
          Look at this. Huh? Nice, yes?

He takes a bottle of whiskey, places it on the desk.

Bizimungu picks up the bottle, takes a swig. He opens the
curtains, peers outside to the courtyard.

                    PAUL (CONT'D)
          The rebels are getting closer, yes?

                    GENERAL BIZIMUNGU
          The rebels can have this graveyard.
          We have ordered everyone out of the
          city. Here. Have a drink.

He hands Paul the bottle of whiskey. Paul takes the bottle,
a swig.

                    GENERAL BIZIMUNGU (CONT'D)
          You know what the Scottish call it?

                    PAUL
          No.

                    GENERAL BIZIMUNGU
          Ishca Baha -- the water of life. I
          went once on a tour of the finest
          distillery in the world. Have you
          ever been to Scotland?

Paul continues to load booze, anxious to get out of there.

                    PAUL
          No, sir.

                    GENERAL BIZIMUNGU
          Wonderful country. Wonderful golf.
          I wonder -- will I ever go back?
          What do you think?

                    PAUL
          No.

Bizimungu looks at him, Paul now pays attention.

                    PAUL (CONT'D)
          I hope we all get to do a great
          many things General. Can we go
          now, please, sir?

> GENERAL BIZIMUNGU
> I'm going to do you a great favor,
> Paul.

A soldier arrives at the door.

> GENERAL BIZIMUNGU (CONT'D)
> Private.

> SOLDIER
> Yes, sir?

> GENERAL BIZIMUNGU
> Pack those carefully in my jeep and
> guard them.

The soldier picks up a crate.

> GENERAL BIZIMUNGU (CONT'D)
> I am going to take you with us, to
> our new headquarters in Gitarama.

> PAUL
> I do not want to go to Gitarama,
> sir.

> GENERAL BIZIMUNGU
> Well, you cannot go back to the
> hotel. The crazy men are on their
> way now.

Paul is now terrified!

> PAUL
> Sir...General, we must go back --
> so that I can get my family.

> GENERAL BIZIMUNGU
> Trust me -- we are better off here.

The General, drinks more.

> PAUL
> General...these are difficult
> times. We need to help one
> another.

> GENERAL BIZIMUNGU
> And what help can I get from you,
> Paul?

> PAUL
> You are a marked man, sir.

                        GENERAL BIZIMUNGU
            How so?

                        PAUL
            You are on the list. The Americans
            have you on their list as a war
            criminal.

                        GENERAL BIZIMUNGU
            Paul, I am sick and tired of your
            lies.

                        PAUL
            Are you stupid, General? How do
            you think these people operate?
            You sit here with five stars on
            your chest, who do you think they
            are coming after?

Bizimungu shakes his head NO.

                        PAUL (CONT'D)
            Fine. We will go to Gitarama --
            and you will stay on that list.

                        GENERAL BIZIMUNGU
            I committed no war crimes.

                        PAUL
            Who will tell them? You need me to
            tell them how you helped at the
            hotel. They blame you for all
            their misfortunes. They said you
            led the massacres.

                        GENERAL BIZIMUNGU
                    (angrily)
            I led no massacres.

                        PAUL
            Do you think they're going to
            believe you?

                        GENERAL BIZIMUNGU
            You will tell the truth!

                        PAUL
            I will do nothing unless you help
            me.

Bizimungu reaches for his pistol.

> PAUL (CONT'D)
> What, what are you going to do,
> shoot me? Shoot me. Please, shoot
> me, it will be a blessing. I will
> pay you -- to shoot my family. You
> cannot hurt me.

Bizimungu grabs Paul's collar.

> GENERAL BIZIMUNGU
> You will tell them I did nothing!

Paul pushes him away.

> PAUL
> We are leaving. Right now.

EXT. HOTEL MILLE COLLINES - ENTRANCE - DAY

The jeep passes through Interahamwe hurrying up the driveway.

Militia swarm around the front of the hotel. The jeeps race
through, scattering them.

Bizimungu points his pistol into the air, shoots. BANG!

> GENERAL BIZIMUNGU
> Get these people away from the
> gate!

INT. HOTEL MILLE COLLINES - HALLWAY - DAY

The Interahamwe are looting the hotel and pushing the
refugees into a huddled group.

> INTERAHAMWE MAN
> Get out! Sit down!

EXT. HOTEL MILLE COLLINES - ENTRANCE - DAY

Bizimungu's jeep reaches the front door, screeches to a halt.
Several refugees sit, huddled and battered. Bizimungu looks
at the Interahamwe looters.

> GENERAL BIZIMUNGU
> Stop it! Stop it! Clear the
> hotel!

Paul does not wait for the hotel to be cleared -- he rushes
in to find his family.

> PAUL
>
> Tatiana!

> GENERAL BIZIMUNGU
>
> Get out of here! Get out! All of
> the Militia must leave now! Get
> out!

INT. HOTEL MILLE COLLINES - LOBBY - DAY

Paul races into the hotel, past frightened refugees who are
being herded outside.

INT. HOTEL MILLE COLLINES - HALLWAY - DAY

He makes it to his floor, pushing past refugees who race down
the stairs.

INT. HOTEL MILLE COLLINES - PAUL'S ROOM - DAY

Paul bursts in. The place is a mess. And it's empty! He
runs to the bathroom, it is also empty. Now he is terrified,
he remembers what he said about the roof.

> PAUL
>
> Oh, no, no!

INT. HOTEL MILLE COLLINES - HALLWAY - DAY

He careens out of the room.

And sees Gregoire coming with a group of Militia!

Then Gregoire notices Paul.

> GREGOIRE
>
> That's him! That's him!

All eyes are on Paul.

> PAUL
> (softly)
> Shit.

> GREGOIRE
>
> That's the manager!

Paul spins around, runs.

GREGOIRE (CONT'D)
Stop him, stop him!

An Interahamwe man grabs Paul.

INTERAHAMWE MAN
I got him! I got him!

Gregoire and the Interahamwe men push through the fleeing
refugees to get to Paul.

Then a roar of gunfire. The ceiling and walls around
Gregoire explode. Showers them with dust.

General Bizimungu's men burst in firing into the air.

HUTU SOLDIER
Get out!

Gregoire and the Interahamwe men are stopped. Paul runs to
the stairs.

EXT. HOTEL MILLE COLLINES - ROOF - DAY

Paul bursts onto the roof.

He runs to the edge of the roof, looks over.

SEES bodies -- women and children, still, on the ground
beneath by a row of hedge.

PAUL
(screams in agony)
Tatiana! Tatiana!

The bodies move, look up. It's not them. It's refugees
hiding, and a woman gestures to Paul -- QUIET.

Paul, delirious with fear, runs along the parapet to Xavier.

PAUL
Have you seen Tatiana?

XAVIER
No, I've not seen Tatiana. Paul,
what is happening, Paul?

PAUL
No, no, no, I have to find my wife.

Below he sees soldiers herding the Militia.

He runs back to the stairs.

INT. HOTEL MILLE COLLINES - HALLWAY - DAY

Soldiers are chasing off the Militia. Paul runs down the
hall, calls out.

                    PAUL
          Tatiana?

INT. HOTEL MILLE COLLINES - PAUL'S ROOM - DAY

Paul staggers in, crazed with fear. He looks under the bed.

From the bathroom he hears a whimper, goes to investigate.

INT. HOTEL MILLE COLLINES - PAUL'S BATHROOM - DAY

He moves over, pulls back the shower curtain.

REVEALS a cluster of women and children, the old ones holding
their hands over the mouths of the young ones.

Tatiana is clutching the shower head like a gun. She
screams. Paul grabs it.

                    PAUL
          They've gone. They've gone.
          They've gone.

Tears, hugs, women tremble.

Paul gestures with the shower head.

                    PAUL (CONT'D)
          What were you going to do with
          this?

                    TATIANA
               (laughs)
          I don't know.

                    PAUL
          I thought you had...

He slumps down against the tile.

                    PAUL (CONT'D)
          ...I thought you had jumped.

Tatiana leans to him -- kisses his cheek.

EXT. HOTEL MILLE COLLINES - ENTRANCE - DAY

Colonel Oliver is with a convoy of UN trucks parked in the forecourt.

Tutsi refugees file up and are helped on board by UN soldiers.

Paul helps Tatiana and the children onto a truck.

Everyone is loaded on the trucks. Paul locks the hotel doors, looks across the deserted lobby.

>   PAUL
>   I hope someday we will come back.

>   OLIVER (O.S.)
>   Let's move out. All right, all
>   right, let's go.

INT. UN TRUCK - DAY

The refugees are crammed inside the truck.

Odette and Jean Baptiste sit with a sick girl between them.

>   PAUL
>   What is wrong with her?

>   ODETTE
>   She has a very high fever.

Tatiana sits with the children, Paul takes her hand.

>   DIANE
>   Where are we going, Daddy?

>   PAUL
>   Some place safe.

EXT. KIGALI STREETS - DAY

The convoy passes through.

A great mass of Hutus fill the road -- Militia, kids, soldiers discarding uniforms.

No longer a mob, but a crush of Hutu refugees no longer
fleeing toward them, fleeing from the advancing of the rebel
army.

INT. UN TRUCK - DAY

Paul looks from the truck at the Hutu refugees as they rumble
through an enormous mass of people. Tens of thousands. One
woman kneels over a man's body, sobbing uncontrollably.

                    PAUL
          My God.

EXT. KIGALI COUNTRY ROAD - DAY

A militiaman throws a bomb into a building. BOOM! Paul
stands up, sees the Interahamwe approaching.

INT. UN TRUCK - DAY

He turns to his family.

                    PAUL
          Everyone, get down! Children, on
          the ground. Bring the children
          this way.

The others pass the children into the back.

                    PAUL (CONT'D)
          Pass them back. Pass them back.

EXT. KIGALI COUNTRY ROADS - DAY

In front of the truck, a militiaman is dragging a machete
along the ground. Inside the jeep Colonel Oliver draws his
gun.

                    OLIVER
          Do not stop. Do not stop. Drive
          right on through.

INT. UN TRUCK - DAY

The orphans in Paul's truck begin crying. It becomes
infectious, spreading to Paul's children and some of the
women.

EXT. KIGALI COUNTRY ROAD - DAY

A gang of Militia men.

They're running fast toward the truck, some carry rifles.

There's more gunfire behind.

The Militia are almost upon the trucks now.

INT. UN TRUCK - DAY

Paul huddles with his family as they kneel on the floor.

> PAUL
> Stay down, stay down.

EXT. COUNTRY ROAD - DAY

The Militia advance.

Then a platoon of Tutsi rebel soldiers, in bush camouflage and red and blue headbands, burst from the brush.

Pursuing, careful, professional. They open fire on the Hutu Militia, killing many.

INT. UN TRUCK - DAY

Chaos. Everyone is terrified. But the gunfire starts to recede. Paul gets up to take a look, sees the rebel soldiers!

> PAUL
> We're crossing the front line.

> 1ST MALE REFUGEE
> It's okay -- we're safe. It's
> okay.

The families start to sit up on the benches. Cheering breaks out. Children frightened again by the sudden euphoria cry.

> 2ND MALE REFUGEE
> It's okay, we are safe now.

EXT. REFUGEE CAMP - DAY

The trucks crawl into the chaos of this massive refugee camp,
a mass of refugees, the wounded, lost children, abandoned old
people, hundreds crammed together.

Paul, Tatiana and the others clamber off the trucks. They
hug, cry, an outpouring of relief.

Colonel Oliver helps the refugees off the trucks.

                    OLIVER
            We made it. Come on, let's get
            down.

AID workers walk towards the trucks to help the refugees.
Paul picks up the sick girl, hands her to Colonel Oliver.

                    PAUL
            She is sick.

                    COLONEL OLIVER
            Okay.

Oliver hands the girl to a Red Cross worker.

                    COLONEL OLIVER (CONT'D)
            Yeah, she's very sick.

Oliver helps Paul down.

                    COLONEL OLIVER
            Paul. The buses are on the other
            side of camp. They'll take you to
            Tanzania. Go now, Paul, 'cos -- I
            don't know when there's gonna be
            another opportunity.

An AID worker helps Dube from the truck, who helps a nun.

Oliver shakes Paul's hand.

                    COLONEL OLIVER
             Good luck.

                    PAUL
             Thank you.

Paul, Tatiana and their children move through the crush of
refugees.

                    PAUL
          Thank God.

                    ODETTE
          We made it, Paul.

                    FEMALE REFUGEE
          Thank you, Paul -- Thank you.

                    PAUL
          Yes, we have made it. Yes, yes.
          Come, come.

Paul urges them to the buses.

                    STEVEN (CONT'D)
          I just wanna thank you.

                    PAUL
          Of course. Steven, of course.

Tatiana sees a friend, CONSTANCE, runs over. They embrace.

                    TATIANA
          Constance, Constance. Thank God
          you are alive! Oh it's so good to
          see you. Have you seen my brother?
          And his wife? No?

                    CONSTANCE
          No. I am sorry.

Tatiana moves on, more frantic, pushing though the crowds
showing a photo.

                    TATIANA
          Has anyone seen these people?

More heads shake NO.

Elys runs up, points to a wall of children's photographs.

The sign above reads DO YOU KNOW THESE CHILDREN?

                    ELYS
          Mama, come see, quick...

Tatiana rushes toward the boards, pushes past refugees.

                    TATIANA
          Excuse me, excuse me.

She frantically searches the boards.

ELYS
Can you see them anywhere?

Tatiana thinks she sees something, then realizes it's not them. She continues through the refugee camp, showing the photo of the girls.

TATIANA
Do you recognize these people?
This little girl, she's Anais, and
this is Carine.

More NOs.

Paul rushes through the crowd, showing the same photograph. People shake heads NO.

PAUL
Ma'am, have you seen these girls?

Paul and Tatiana continue searching as they move inexorably toward the buses. Time's running out.

TATIANA
Anais. And that's my brother.

AID WORKER (O.S.)
On the buses, please. Everybody on
the buses.

UN soldiers are ushering refugees onto the buses.

INT. REFUGEE CAMP - RED CROSS TENT - DAY

Wounded refugees -- men, women, children. Then a woman appears. It's Pat, treating the injured.

TANNOY (O.S.)
Everybody, on the buses.

EXT. REFUGEE CAMP - DAY

Refugees climb onto the buses. Paul and family in line.

PAUL
We'll find the girls, Tatsi.

TATIANA
Yes.

                        PAUL
          We will.

INT. REFUGEE CAMP - RED CROSS TENT - DAY

A new group of injured children is carried in. Pat
recognizes the sick girl from the truck, rushes over.

                        PAT ARCHER
               Moussey?

She joyously embraces and holds the young orphan.

                        PAT ARCHER (CONT'D)
                    (softly)
               It's you.

Pat looks to the MEDIC who brought her in.

                        PAT ARCHER (CONT'D)
               Where'd you find this child?

                        MEDIC
               They just arrived on trucks from
               the Mille Collines.

Pat hurries out of the tent.

EXT. REFUGEE CAMP - DAY

Refugees are lining up outside the Red Cross tent to get
treatments. Pat rushes outside, looks wildly around.

                        TANNOY (O.S.)
               All the Mille Collines refugees to
               the buses now please.

She sees the buses begin to pull away.

                        PAT ARCHER
               Oh no.

INT. BUS - DAY

Odette, Jean Baptiste and the refugees are seated on the bus
as it pulls off.

Tatiana and Paul sit down.

EXT. REFUGEE CAMP - DAY

Pat sees the buses leaving.

The throng of refugees is moving slowly towards the buses.
Pat pushes through them, runs fast.

> PAT ARCHER
> Wait! Hold it, please!

The bus is still moving. Now she sees Tatiana. She bangs
her hand against the window.

> PAT ARCHER (CONT'D)
> Tatiana!

INT. BUS - DAY

Tatiana sits with her family. Exhausted, she leans against
the window. BANG!

She looks out, sees Pat.

> TATIANA
> It's Pat! Pat!

Paul stands, leans toward the window.

> PAT ARCHER
> Tatiana!

> PAUL
> Madame Archer!
> (to driver)
> Stop the bus!

The bus stops and Paul leads his family off.

EXT. BUS - DAY

Paul climbs down from the bus.

Paul reaches Pat. They embrace.

> PAUL
> (chuckles) Madame Archer. I was
> so worried. I thought...it's
> wonderful to see you.

                        PAT ARCHER
          Come quickly.

Pat leads Paul and his family into a holding area for
children, to a makeshift kitchen serving food to a line of
orphaned children.

Paul and Tatiana rush down the line, studying each child's
face. They search for the girls, calling their names.

                        TATIANA
          Carine! Carine!

                        PAUL
          Anais!

                        TATIANA
          Anais!

                        AID WORKER (O.S.)
          Just wait. It's gonna be in just a
          minute now.

Even the children, Roger and Elys, are helping. They run
around the groups of children, calling their cousins' names.

                        ROGER
          Anais...Carine.

Tatiana looks to another group of orphans who are singing.
Searches their faces. Then sees something!

                        TATIANA
          Oh my God!

It's Anais and Carine!

                        TATIANA (CONT'D)
          Oh, thank God!

She rushes to the girls. Throws her arms around them, lifts
Anais.

Paul runs up, embraces the girls.

                        PAUL
          (chuckles) Girls. Hello darling.
          Anais, hello, how are you,
          sweetheart?

                        ELYS (O.S.)
          Oh, I've missed you so much.

> PAUL
> Do you see your cousins?

They walk back towards the buses with Pat. Tatiana and Paul
lead their children. They have Anais and Carine in their
arms. Pat now has her little group of orphans.

> PAT ARCHER
> They said there wasn't any room.

> PAUL
> There's always room.

Their laughter mixes with tears of joy as they reach a bus.

> FADE TO BLACK.

Paul Rusesabagina sheltered 1268 Tutsi and Hutu refugees at
the Mille Collines Hotel in Kigali.

Paul and Tatiana now live in Belgium with their children,
Roger, Diane, Lys, Tresor, and their adopted nieces Anais and
Carina.

Tatiana's brother Thomas and his wife Fedens were never
found.

In 2002, General Augustin Bizimungu was captured in Angola
and transported to the U.N. War Crimes Tribunal in Tanzania.
At the same tribunal, the Interahamwe leader George Rutagunda
was sentenced to life in prison.

The genocide ended in July 1994, when the Tutsi rebels drove
the Hutu army and the Interahamwe militia across the border
into the Congo.

Cast and Crew Credits

UNITED ARTISTS presents in association with LIONS GATE ENTERTAINMENT
a SOUTH AFRICA/UNITED KINGDOM/ITALY co-production in association
with THE INDUSTRIAL DEVELOPMENT CORPORATION OF SOUTH AFRICA
a MIRACLE PICTURES/SEAMUS production
produced in association with INSIDE TRACK

A film by TERRY GEORGE

HOTEL RWANDA

DON CHEADLE   SOPHIE OKONEDO   JOAQUIN PHOENIX and NICK NOLTE

Co-Producers
Bridget Pickering
Luigi Musini

Co-Executive Producers
Keir Pearson
Nicolas Meyer

Consultant
Paul Rusesabagina

Executive Producers
Hal Sadoff
Martin F. Katz
Duncan Reid
Sam Bhembe

Music
Andrea Guerra
Rupert Gregson-Williams
Afro Celt Sound System

Costume Designer
Ruy Filipe

Editor
Naomi Geraghty

Production Designers
Tony Burrough
Johnny Breedt

Director of Photography
Robert Fraisse

Produced by
A. Kitman Ho
Terry George

Written by
Keir Pearson & Terry George

Directed by
Terry George

CAST (in order of appearance)
POLICEMAN . . . . XOLANI MALI
PAUL RUSESABAGINA . . . . . . DON CHEADLE
DUBE. . . . . DESMOND DUBE
GEORGE RUTAGUNDA. . HAKEEM KAE-KAZIM
GREGOIRE . . . . TONY KGOROGE
RECEPTIONIST. . . . . ROSIE MOTENE
JEAN JACQUES. . . . . NEIL McCARTHY
HEAD CHEF. . . . . KID SITHOLE
COLONEL OLIVER. . . . . NICK NOLTE
GENERAL BIZIMUNGU . . . . FANA MOKOENA
OLD GUARD. . . . . JEREMIAH NDLOVU
TATIANA RUSESABAGINA . . SOPHIE OKONEDO
ODETTE. . . . . LEBO MASHILE
THOMAS MIRAMA . . ANTONIO DAVID LYONS
FEDENS . . . . LELETI KHUMALO
ANAIS . . . . KGOMOTSO SEITSHOHLO
CARINE . . . . LERATO MOKGOTHO
ELYS RUSESABAGINA . . . . . . MOSA KAISER
DIANE RUSESABAGINA. . MATHABO PIETERSON

ROGER RUSESABAGINA. . OFENTSE MODISELLE
DAVID . . . . DAVID O'HARA
JACK DAGLISH . . . . JOAQUIN PHOENIX
PETER . . . . LENNOX MATHABATHE
BENEDICT . . . . MOTHUSI MAGANO
CHLOE (PROSTITUTE). . . . .
NOXOLO MAQASHALALA
JEAN BAPTISTE . . . . THULANE NYEMBE
HUTU CAPTAIN. . . . . SIMO MAGWAZA
GREGOIRE'S GIRLFRIEND . . . .
MIRRIAM NGOMANI
PAT ARCHER . . . . CARA SEYMOUR
ALICE THE WAITRESS. . HARRIET MANAMELA
PRIEST. . . . . ROBERTO CITRAN
HUTU LIEUTENANT . . . . MDUDUZI MABASO
MILITIAMAN. . . . . SONNI CHIDIEBERE
XAVIER. . . . . THOMAS KARIUKI
MILITIAMAN . . . . SIBUSISO MHLONGO
MEDIC. . . . . ASHLEIGH TOBIAS

CREW

Stunt Coordinator . . . . GRAHAM PRESS
Unit Production Manager . . . . . . A. KITMAN HO
1st Assistant Director . . . . . . LIONEL STEKETEE
2nd Assistant Director . . . . ALEXANDER OAKLEY

In Association with Endgame Entertainment Fund I, LLC

Second Unit Directed by . . . . A. KITMAN HO

Supervising Sound Editor . . . . NIGEL MILLS
Re-Recording Sound Mixers . . . . TOM JOHNSON
    DOUGLAS COOPER
Production Sound Mixer . . . . . . JOHN MIDGLEY
Casting. . . . . RICK PAGANO
    MOONYEENN LEE
Post-Production Consultant. . . . . ARTURO SOSA
Production Manager (Kigali). . OORLAGH GEORGE
Art Director . . . . EMMA MacDEVITT
Set Decorator . . . . ESTELLE (FLO) BALLACK
A Camera Operator . . . . KEVIN JEWISON
B Camera Operator/Steadicam . . DEON VERMEULEN
Additional Footage Cameraman . . . .
    VINCENT G. COX, ASC., SASC., BSC(F)
A Camera Focus . . . . LARS COX
B Camera Focus . . . . ANTON WEHMEYER
A Camera Loader . . . . SHANI HAYWARD
B Camera Loader . . . . TROY LEE
Loader . . . . DEREK UECKERMANN
Stills Photographer . . . . . KARIN BLID ALSBIRK
Special Stills . . . . FRANK CONNOR
Script Supervisor. . . . . LISA VICK
Special Projects Consultant . . . . . M.J. MAGBANUA
Production Coordinator . . . . ELAINE BURT
Production Accountant . . . ALISTAIR THOMPSON
Chief Lighting Technician . . . . . BRUCE THOMAS
Assistant Lighting Technician . . . MARK SHERMAN
Electricians . . . . SIMON CAVE
    EMMANUEL CHONCO
    ALFRED MANZINI
Genny Operator . . . . GODFREY NKESE
Key Grip . . . . CHARL PHYFER
2nd Company Grip . . . . KENNETH SHANGE
Grips . . . . WESLEY WILLIAMS
    PATRICK MASHILO
Unit Manager . . . . HENDRIK H. SPANGENBERG
Assistant Unit Manager
    RENIER GERHARD CORDIER
Location Manager . . . . BRUCE THACKWELL
Location Assistant. . . . . DANIELLE GIA VINOKUR

Basecamp Manager . . . . DARRYL KRUGER
2nd 2nd Assistant Directors . . . . LANCE ROEHRIG
    CARIN DE KOCK
    CHRISTIAN VAN LATUM
Assistant Editors . . . . LISA CLIFFORD OWEN
    CHRISTELLE NICOLE VAN NIEKERK
Sound Effects Editor . . . . ANDY KENNEDY
Dialogue Editor . . . . NIGEL STONE
ADR Editors . . . . NICK LOWE
    CONOR MACKEY
Foley Editor . . . . MIKE WOOD
Assistant Sound Editor . . . . . EMILY REYNOLDS
Foley Artists . . . . ANDI DERRICK
    PETER BURGESS
ADR Mixer . . . . ANDY THOMPSON
Foley Mixers . . . . PAUL CARR
    MARK PATERSON
Voice Casting . . . . BRENDAN DONNISON, MPSE
    VANESSA BAKER
Post-Production Supervisor . . . ALISTAIR HOPKINS
Post-Production Coordinator . . VERITY WISLOCKI
Post-Production Accountant . . . . . DAVID MELLOR
Boom Operators . . . . JUNE PRINZ
    DAVID SUTTON
Sound Assistant . . . . ANNELINE DE KOCK
Music Editor . . . . MICHAEL CONNELL

Wardrobe Mistress. . . . . PETA HUNTER
Wardrobe . . . . MELANIE FINCH
    TAMLIN FRENCH
    JOHANNES CHRISTIAN VORSTER
Pattern Cutter . . . . MATHILDA ENGELBRECHT
Wardrobe Assistants . . . . . . ZELLE BOREJSZO,
    MELANIE LUBBE, NATASHA T. STEVENS, ADA
    MEYER, THEMBI FAITH MADLALA, SHELELE
    SEKHU, NATALIE LUNDON, MELISSA GATES
Seamstresses. . . . . BRENDA MOGALE
    ROSE NTOMBI PARKER
    ZAHELE RATHLEPE
    SANNAH HAPPY DEDIBE
Wardrobe Runner . . . . WARREN VAN NIEKERK
Chief Make-Up Artist . . . . . SUZANNE BELCHER
Make-Up Artist . . . . TANIA BROOKE
Crowd Make-Up . . . . ANGIE BOSHOFF
Make-Up Assistant, Extras . . . . . MARLI KRUGER
Make-Up Assistants . . . . . . MELISSA SLABBERT
    LIANNE SCOTT
    GLADYS TSHIDI PHOKOMPE
Chief Hairdresser . . SUZANNE STOKES-MUNTON
Crowd Hairdresser . . . . JACQUES GERBER

Hair Assistant . . . . CHARLES KHOZA
Prop Masters . . . . BRYN GEORGE
                          RALF BUCHMANN
Stand-by Props . . . . BOB TOMS
Armoury. . . . . BRUCE WENTZEL
                  MICHAEL DAVID DRISCOLL
Art Department Coordinator. . . . TAMZIN ELLETT
Props Buyer . . . . JAMES LEE TAYLOR
Props . . . . BHEKI MNCUBE
Assistant Stand by . . . . SAMSON SITOLE
Storyboard Artist/Draughtsman . . . . RAY BERMAN
Draughtsmen. . . . . . . HERTZOG SCHALEKAMP
                        SHIRA HOCKMAN
Stand-by Set Dressers . . . . . . GEORGE NDLOVU
Assistant Set Dresser. . . . . VICKY SAWKINS
Set Dressers . . . . THOMAS POTSANE
                        ARCHIBALD NKOSI
                        ISAAC TSOTETSI
                    WINSTON MAZIBUKO
                        ASHLEIGH TOBIAS
                      BONGANI LEDWABA
Construction Manager . . . RAYMOND G. MULLER
Construction Foremen . . . . LOUIS MARAIS
                      GRAHAM DERROCKS
Construction Supervisor . . . .
          KEITH RICARDO VAN DER VENT
Construction . . . . . . MOHAMMED HOOSAIN
Construction Assistant . . . . . ALFRED MKWANAZI
Construction Runner   MARLON BRANDO MACKS
Storemen . . . . KERWIN MACKS
                            RALPH SMIT
Head Scenic . . . .
         HERMANUS (FOURIE) ACKERMANN
Scenics . . . . MARSHA HOLTZHAUSEN
                         RICHARD NTULI
Scenic Artist . . . . MELINDA LAUNSPACH
Welder / Rigger. . . PIETER WILLEM KLEINHAUS
Stand-by Carpenter . . . . . . BRENDAN GIFFORD
Greensman. . . . . MITCH GORDON
Greens Assistants . . . . PAUL BARKER
                     MICHAEL JOHN LAW
Assistant Greensman . . . . JULIAN STOBBS
Special Effects Supervisor. . . . . GAVIN MEADON
Special Effects Coordinator . . . DAVID MAHLANGU
Transport Manager . . . . SEAN BERKHOUT
Transport Coordinators . . . . LESIBA JOE MPHELA
                        JANNIE VISSER
Action Vehicles Coordinators. . . PIETER DE LANGE
                         JIMMY DAVIES
Assistant Coordinator . . STEVEN DAVID CLAYTON

Action Vehicle Assistant. . . . . EUGENE KOK
On Set Mechanic . . . . HENDRIK WHITE
Drivers . . . . ALBERT MAPHOSHO,
     GABRIEL MACHABA, ELIAS MAKHANYA,
                      HODGES SIBEKO
Producer's Representative . . . . ARTHUR MANSON
Unit Publicist . . . . STEVEN MARESCH – METAL
         MOON MARKETING (PTY) LTD
Publicity Consultant . . . . ROB HARRIS
1st Assistant Accountant . . . . JANE TROWER
Assistant Accountant. . . . . FELICITY DOWNING
Post-Production Assistant Accountant . . . .
                          HUGO MELLOR
Assistants to Terry George . . . . CHER BUDD
                  BRIAN LETLHABANE
                  DANNY WIMBORNE
Assistant to Don Cheadle . . . . . . NATALIE HOOK
Assistant to Sophie Okonedo . . . .
          VINCENT THUSO PANENG
Assistants to Nick Nolte . . . . MATT POLISH
                    BRAWLEY NOLTE
Production Runners. . . . . CHERYL EATOCK
                     JOSEPH MALELE
Production Travel. . . . . LEIGH HUMAN
Production Accommodation . . . JANINE WILLIAMS
Production Office Craft. . . . . DIANA SIKHOSANA
Assistant Production Coordinators. . . . .
     CIARA McGOWAN, JANA ERASMUS
Assistant Production Coordinator, Kigali . . . .
                      RAYMOND KALISA
Accounts Assistant . . . . . . RETHA GELDENHUYS
Cashier . . . . MELVIN VAN ROSS
Dialect Coaches . . . . FIONA RAMSAY
                     LEON MORENZIE
Tutor . . . . NANIE TAYLOR
Army Advisor . . . . BOB GIBSON
Crowd Coordinator . . . . DAVID WILLIAMS
Assistant Crowd Coordinator. . . . . CLAIR EVANS
Production Assistant . . . . . . CLARIBEL NKWILI
Production Assistant, Kigali . . . . . PAUL KAMERA
Props Assistant . . . . THERON RAMATLADI
Art Department Runners . . . . JAMES RYAN
        MARINA HELENA CONSTANDSE
Video Assist Trainee . . . . PETER SEKELE
Training Coordinator. . . . . SELLO MOLEFE
Script Supervisor's Trainee . . . . . . DUMA NKOSI
Sound Trainee . . . . ASHLEY SEALE
Editing Trainee . . . . THATO SEGOTO
Assistant Director Trainee . . . . . VINCENT MOLOI
Production Trainee. . . . . NEO RAPHOTO

Wardrobe Trainee . . . . . . VIVIENNE MAHLOKO
Medics . . . . GERT CORDIER
         NICHOLAS FINEGAN
         JANICE FINEGAN
Security . . . . THOSA SECURITY
Visual Effects . . . . BASEBLACK LTD
Visual Effects Supervisor, Lead 3D . . VAL WARDLAW
Visual Effects Producer . . . . STEPHEN ELSON
Senior Compositors . . . . . MICHAEL CONNOLLY
         PAUL POETSCH
Senior Compositor, Effects Animator . . . .
         CHRIS PANTON
Compositors . . . . PETRA SCHWANE
         DONAL NOLAN
Sys Admin, R . . . . JOHN KOZAK
3D, R . . . . PER KAREFELT
Visual Effects Coordinator . . . . . . CLARE TINSLEY
Studio Manager . . . . LYNDY BROWN
For Ingenious Films
Physical Production . . . . PAULA JALFON
Legal . . . . ALISON BRISTER
         LESLEY WISE

THE PRODUCERS WISH TO THANK:
Mbhazima Shilowa - Premier of Gauteng Provisional
Government
Mogopodi Mokoena - Director General of Gauteng
Provisional Government
Themba Sibeko of Gauteng Film Office
Basil Ford of The Industrial Development Corporation
of South Africa
Zama Mkosi of The Industrial Development Corporation
of South Africa
Khalipha Edward Mbalo of The National Film and Video
Foundation of South Africa
The People of Alexandra and
Thembisa, Johannesburg, S.A.
In Kigali, Rwanda:
Odette Nyiramilimo & Jean Baptiste Gasisira
Jean de Dieu Ntiruhungwa
Anita Haguma
Joseph Demali
Part of the profits from this film shall go to
The Rwandese Survivors Fund

Music
Music Supervisors . . Becky Bentham and Becca Gatrell
for Hot°House Music
Andrea Guerra's Compositions:

Musical Production . . . . . . Sud Ovest Records Srl
Performed by . Bulgarian Symphony Orchestra - Sif 309
Conducted by . . . . Gianfranco Plenizio
Orchestration . . . . Andrea Guerra
         Luca Salvadori
Ethnic Woods Soloist . . . . Mario Crispi
Choir . . . . Coro da camera del C.I.M.A.
Midi Programming . . . . Tony Puia
Maestro Assistant . . . . Giannandrea Mazza
Recording Studios . . . . Studio 1 BNR (Sofia)
         Forum Music Village (Roma)
Mixing Studio . . . . . . Forum Music Village (Roma)
Sound Engineer . . . . Marco Streccioni
Assistant Engineers . . . . Vladislav Boiadjiev
         Attilio Tucci
Pro Tools Operator . . . . Damiano Antinori
'Tall Trees' Featured Vocals by . . Dorothee Munyaneza
Rupert Gregson-Williams' Compositions:
Music Mixed by . . . . Guy Fletcher at A-Bay Studios
Programming by . . . . Christian Henson
         Lorne Balfe
Additional Arrangements by . . . . Alastair King
Track Laying by . . . . Simon Changer

Umqombothi
Written by Attie van Wyk & Chicco Twala
Performed by Yvonne Chaka Chaka
Published by Universal Music Publishing Ltd on behalf
of Tela Music
Courtesy of Universal Records

Olugendo Lw'e Bulaya
Written by Bernard Kabanda
Published by Real World Works Ltd
Produced and recorded binaurally by Tchad Blake at
Real World Studios
(P) 1999 Real World Records Ltd
From the WOMAD Select album 'Olugendo' WSCD106

Whispered Song with inanga accompaniment
CD Ocora C559003
Burundi: Musiques Traditionelles (Track 1)

Ubuhuha
CD Ocora C559003
Burundi: Musiques Traditionelles (Trks 3 and 4)

Ikibo
Arranged by Dorothee & Faith Munyaneza

Mwali we!
Arranged & Performed by Dorothee & Benjamin
Munyaneza

At The Warehouse
Hutu Power Re-Visited
Lobsters Pt1
Poolside Muzak
Lobsters Pt2
Sorrow
The Chosen
All Written by Afro Celt Sound System (Emmerson/
McNally/ O'Lionaird/ Russell)
Published by Real World Music Ltd
Arranged, Produced, Engineered & Mixed by Martin
Russell at Sonic Innovation 2 / UK
(P) 2004 Afro Celt Sound System appear courtesy of
Real World Records Ltd

Mama Ararira
Yariz' Ampeka
All Written by Dorothee Munyaneza/ Afro Celt Sound
System (Emmerson/ McNally/ O'Lionaird/ Russell)
Published by Real World Music Ltd
Arranged, Produced, Engineered & Mixed by Martin
Russell at Sonic Innovation 2 / UK
Real World Records Ltd
(P) 2004 Afro Celt Sound System appear courtesy of
Real World Records Ltd

Script Clearances. . . . .
    JOAN PEARCE RESEARCH ASSOCIATES
                    ASHLEY KRAVITZ
Post-Production Sound Services. . . . .
    GOLDCREST POST PRODUCTION, LONDON
Title Design & Optical Effects . . . . . . CAPITAL FX
Neg Cutter. PNC
Insurance. . . . . AON / ALBERT G. RUBEN
                    INSURANCE SERVICES
Completion Guarantor . . . . . . FILM FINANCES
Payroll Services . . SARGENT-DISC LTD., LONDON
Auditors. . . . . MALDE & CO.
Collection Account Management . FINTAGE HOUSE
Legal Affairs. . . . . OLSWANG
Camera Equipment . . PANACAM, AFRICA (Pty) Ltd.
Grips Equipment . . . . . MCC LOGICAL DESIGNS
Lighting Equipment . . . .
    AFM LIGHTING, SOUTH AFRICA (PTY)
Video Equipment . . . . LIQUID STUDIO
Film Stock . . . . KODAK

THE MOVIE CAMERA COMPANY
Laboratories . . . .
    THE FILM LAB, JHB TECHNICOLOR, UK
Telecine . . . . THE VIDEO LAB

INSIDE TRACK θ

Financing Provided by Bank Leumi

A Kigali Releasing Ltd Production for Inside Track 1LLP

Filmed on location in Kigali, Rwanda and Johannesburg,
South Africa

Visit the **United Artists** Website at:
WWW.UNITEDARTISTS.COM

DISTRIBUTED BY MGM DISTRIBUTION CO.

PG-13	PARENTS STRONGLY CAUTIONED
Some Material May Be Inappropriate for Children Under 13	
VIOLENCE, DISTURBING IMAGES AND BRIEF STRONG LANGUAGE	

Running time: 121 minutes

Bios

TERRY GEORGE (Director/Writer/Producer) received Academy Award®, and BAFTA nominations for his first produced screenplay, *In the Name of the Father*. His directorial debut, *Some Mother's Son*, won awards at the European Film Festival, Angers European First Film Festival, and the San Sebastian International Film Festival. George was named European Young Director of the Year in 1996.

George subsequently adapted and directed the acclaimed HBO movie based on Neil Sheehan's Pulitzer Prize-winning Vietnam War tale, *A Bright and Shining Lie*. The feature was honored with Emmy and Golden Globe nominations.

George's other writing credits include the Sheridan-directed drama *The Boxer* starring Daniel Day Lewis, and *Hart's War* starring Bruce Willis and Colin Farrell. He created and produced the CBS drama series *The District*, which was the no. 1 rated TV show on Saturday night for four years.

George lives in Ireland and New York.

KEIR PEARSON (Writer/Co-Executive Producer) worked as a documentary editor from 1995 to 2003, cutting shows for PBS, New York Times Television, and Court TV. *Hotel Rwanda* is his first feature writing credit.

He received his Bachelor of Arts from Harvard College in 1990 and a Masters in Fine Arts from NYU Film School in 1997.

Pearson is an Olympic athlete. He competed in the 1992 Olympics in Barcelona, Spain, as a member of the U.S.A. Rowing Team.

A. KITMAN HO (Producer) is a veteran filmmaker whose credits include the multiple Academy Award®-winning films *JFK*, *Born on the Fourth of July*, *Platoon* and *Wall Street*, all with director

Oliver Stone. Among his other producing credits are Stone's *Heaven and Earth*, *The Doors* and *Talk Radio*. More recently, Ho has produced *Ali*, *The Weight of Water*, *Brokedown Palace*, *The Ghost in the Darkness* and *On Deadly Ground*.

Born in Hong Kong, Ho immigrated with his family to the United States when he was five years old. After graduating from Goddard College with a Masters degree in Cinema, he continued his studies at New York University's Tisch School of the Arts.

Ho began his career as a location manager on the cult hit *The Warriors* and has been involved in all aspects of film production. His first credit as a feature film producer was on Kathryn Bigelow's *The Loveless* in 1983.

Ho's television credits include executive producing the documentary *China: Unleashing the Dragon* and the miniseries *Wild Palms*.

PAUL RUSESABAGINA (Consultant) was born June 15, 1954, at Murama-Gitarama in the Central-South of Rwanda; his parents were farmers. In 1962, he entered the SDA (Seventh Day Adventist) College of Gitwe, a Missionary School, and was there for 13 years (7 years for primary school and 6 years for secondary studies).

From 1975 to 1978, Rusesabagina attended the Faculty of Theology in Cameroon and in January 1979 was employed by Sabena as a front office manager in their newly opened Hotel Akagera in the Akagera National Park. It was at this time he learned about the Tourism, Hotel and Catering Industry.

Through The Suisse Tourist Consult, his application was accepted for entrance into the Kenya Utalii College in Nairobi in the Hotel Management Course, which he started in early 1980 and finished in September 1984 in Switzerland.

Back from Switzerland, Rusesabagina joined Sabena Hotels again and was employed as assistant general manager in the Mille Collines Hotel from October 1984 to November 1993, when he was promoted as general manager of the Diplomat Hotel, which is also in Kigali. Due to regional problems, he was only able to join his new office in March 1993.

For the 100 days of the genocide, Rusesabagina had to move back to the Mille Collines Hotel. His colleague Bik, manager of that unit, left Kigali on April 11, 1994, at 5:00pm, despite the number of refugees still left on their own. It was the next morning, April 12th, when the government (Interim Government) left Kigali for Gitarama. Rusesabagina was there for almost the entire span of the genocide.

When the massacre slightly calmed down, in July 1994, Bik came back and joined his unit, and Rusesabagina went back to the Diplomat Hotel where he stayed until September 1996, after which he went to Belgium as a refugee.

From that time to date, Rusesabagina has worked as a businessman and owns a heavy duty transport company.

DON CHEADLE (Paul) received a Golden Globe award for his remarkable portrayal of Sammy Davis, Jr., in HBO's *The Rat Pack*. His feature films include *Ocean's Eleven*, *Traffic*, *Out of Sight*, *Boogie Nights*, *Bulworth*, *Swordfish*, *Devil in a Blue Dress*, *After the Sunset*, *Ocean's Twelve*, *Crash*, and his upcoming directorial debut, *Tishomingo Blues*.

SOPHIE OKONEDO (Tatiana) has worked on several films, including *Dirty Pretty Things*, for which she was nominated for Best Actress from the Independent Spirit Awards. Her other credits include *Aeon Flux*, *This Year's Love*, *The Jackal*, *Go Now*, *Cross My Heart*, *Mad Bad Mortal Beings*, *Miss Queencake*, and *Young Soul Rebels*.

JOAQUIN PHOENIX (Jack) was nominated for an Academy Award® as well as a Golden Globe for his work in *Gladiator*. His other films include *Russkies, Parenthood, Inventing the Abbotts, U-Turn, 8MM, The Yards, Quills, Signs, The Village, Ladder 49*, and the upcoming *Walk the Line*, in which he stars as country music legend Johnny Cash.

NICK NOLTE (Colonel Oliver), a two-time Academy Award® nominee, has starred in *The Good Thief, The Hulk, Blue Chips, Lorenzo's Oil, The Deep, North Dallas Forty, Down and Out in Beverly Hills, 48 Hours, Q&A, Affliction, U-Turn, Cape Fear*, and *The Prince of Tides*, for which he won a Golden Globe.

Acknowledgments

The publisher Esther Margolis wishes to thank the following for their special contributions to the creation of this book: Terry George, Oorlagh George, and Ronnie Saha at *Hotel Rwanda*; co-writer Keir Pearson; producer Alex Kitman Ho; writers Anne Thompson and Nicola Graydon; at United Artists, Danny Rosett, Rebecca Kearey, Ian Wilson, Craig Greiwe, Sara Finmann, Holly Haines, Monica Guzman, and Karen Painter; and at Newmarket Press, Keith Hollaman, Shannon Berning, Edward McPherson, Paul Sugarman, Frank DeMaio, Harry Burton, and Heidi Sachner.

THE INTERNATIONAL FUND FOR RWANDA

There is an incredible story to be told that begins where *Hotel Rwanda* leaves off, of a country constantly redefining the capacity to rebuild, to learn, and to forgive. The individuals portrayed in the film and the filmmakers have partnered with the United Nations Foundation to create the International Fund for Rwanda, an organization that directly supports humanitarian, development, and survivor programs on the ground in Rwanda. A percentage of the proceeds from *Hotel Rwanda* will go to the International Fund for Rwanda and donations of all shapes and sizes are encouraged. Donations will support the organization on the ground in Rwanda.

For more information and to make a donation please go to www.internationalfundforrwanda.org.

You can learn more and communicate with the individuals portrayed in the film and the filmmakers at www.hotelrwanda.com. To learn more about the United Nations Foundation log on to www.unfoundation.org.